Information Skills

D1125485

www.skills4study.com – the leading study skills website

Palgrave Study Skills

Authoring a PhD
Business Degree Success
Career Skills
Critical Thinking Skills
Cite them Right (8th edn)
e-Learning Skills (2nd edn)
Effective Communication for
  Arts and Humanities Students
Effective Communication for
  Science and Technology
The Exam Skills Handbook
The Foundations of Research (2nd edn)
The Good Supervisor
Great Ways to Learn Anatomy and
  Physiology
How to Manage your Arts, Humanities and
  Social Science Degree
How to Manage your Distance and
  Open Learning Course
How to Manage your Postgraduate Course
How to Manage your Science and
  Technology Degree
How to Study Foreign Languages
How to use your Reading in your Essays
How to Write Better Essays (2nd edn)
How to Write your Undergraduate
  Dissertation
Information Skills
IT Skills for Successful Study
Making Sense of Statistics
The International Student Handbook
The Mature Student's Guide to Writing (2nd edn)
The Mature Student's Handbook
The Palgrave Student Planner
The Personal Tutor's Handbook

The Postgraduate Research Handbook (2nd edn)
Presentation Skills for Students (2nd edn)
The Principles of Writing in Psychology
Professional Writing (2nd edn)
Researching Online
Research Using IT
Skills for Success (2nd edn)
The Study Abroad Handbook
The Student's Guide to Writing (2nd edn)
The Student Life Handbook
The Study Skills Handbook (3rd edn)
Study Skills for Speakers of English as
  a Second Language
Studying Arts and Humanities
Studying the Built Environment
Studying Business at MBA and Masters Level
Studying Economics
Studying History (3rd edn)
Studying Law (2nd edn)
Studying Mathematics and its Applications
Studying Modern Drama (2nd edn)
Studying Physics
Studying Programming
Studying Psychology (2nd edn)
Teaching Study Skills and Supporting Learning
The Undergraduate Research Handbook
The Work-Based Learning Student Handbook
Work Placements – A Survival Guide for Students
Writing for Law
Writing for Nursing and Midwifrey Students
Write it Right
Writing for Engineers (3rd edn)

Palgrave Study Skills: Literature

General Editors: John Peck and Martin Coyle

How to Begin Studying English Literature
  (3rd edn)
How to Study a Jane Austen Novel (2nd edn)
How to Study a Charles Dickens Novel
How to Study Chaucer (2nd edn)
How to Study an E. M. Forster Novel
How to Study James Joyce
How to Study Linguistics (2nd edn)

How to Study Modern Poetry
How to Study a Novel (2nd edn)
How to Study a Poet
How to Study a Renaissance Play
How to Study Romantic Poetry (2nd edn)
How to Study a Shakespeare Play (2nd edn)
How to Study Television
Practical Criticism

Information Skills

Finding and Using the Right Resources

Jonathan Grix
Gerald Watkins

First published 2010 by
PALGRAVE MACMILLAN

Palgrave Macmillan in the UK is an imprint of Macmillan Publishers Limited, registered in England, company number 785998, of Houndmills, Basingstoke, Hampshire RG21 6XS.

Palgrave Macmillan in the US is a division of St Martin's Press LLC, 175 Fifth Avenue, New York, NY 10010.

Palgrave Macmillan is the global academic imprint of the above companies and has companies and representatives throughout the world.

Palgrave® and Macmillan® are registered trademarks in the United States, the United Kingdom, Europe and other countries

ISBN 978–0–230–22250–2

This book is printed on paper suitable for recycling and made from fully managed and sustained forest sources. Logging, pulping and manufacturing processes are expected to conform to the environmental regulations of the country of origin.

A catalogue record for this book is available from the British Library.

10   9   8   7   6   5   4   3   2   1
19 18 17 16 15 14 13 12 11 10

Printed in China

17.00   001.4
          Gri

Contents

Acknowledgements

A number of people need to be thanked for their help, assistance, patience and forbearance during the making of this book. First and foremost, we would like to thank Suzannah Burywood. Jonathan Grix's enjoyable previous experience of working with Suzannah, a publisher at Palgrave, was the reason why we took on this project in the first place. We would also like to thank the illustrator, Sallie Godwin, for so successfully transforming the original concept drawings by an ageing librarian into something more in tune with the modern world. Also, thanks to David Pulford of the University of Birmingham for the original idea of the 'Information Landscape' in Chapter 3, an attempt to use graphic methods to counter death by bullet point in presentations. Thanks, finally, to Palgrave's editorial assistant, Jenni Burnell, whose firm emails ensured we did as we were instructed, thereby keeping the project on schedule.

JONATHAN GRIX AND GERALD WATKINS
March 2010

To Andrea, Lebensgefährtin and wife

Jonathan Grix

In memory of my Mum, Denise

Gerald Watkins

The results of reading *Information Skills*

"Before"
Tangled and confused

"After"
Sorted!

Introduction

The intention of this slim volume is to provide a text that offers students and researchers alike an overview of information skills and best practice in finding resources. Whilst a plethora of texts exist on specific study skills, the research process and particular research techniques, there is no single, short text dedicated to finding resources, and offering sound advice on how to do so. Until now that is. This volume has the advantage of being able to offer a more detailed text on a wide variety of sources, including the ever-expanding online resources available. Our target audience ranges from college students to postgraduates working within the social sciences, or the broader area, human sciences (that is, all subjects that focus on social phenomena; some schools of social sciences, for example, do not include health studies or social geography, subjects we are keen not to leave out).

Universities and colleges in the UK have at their disposal a massive range of academic quality resources – the following chapters show you how to make the most of them. If you do not have access to such resources, we offer insights into how to access and make the best of those that are freely available.

The following offers guidance on the role of, and how to carry out, a review of literature, as well as dealing with online data retrieval. Skills for quickly and accurately finding the correct information are essential for academic study, but are also transferable to life after college or university. Employers need people who can locate and critically assess large volumes of information and present it in a coherent fashion. This is effectively what a literature review does, with the added task of explaining how the student's work relates to the current body of literature. This book can impart the lessons needed to acquire such skills. Both for your studies and for the world of work you will need to be able to evaluate and assess the Internet and distinguish between sources that are of academic quality; those that are non-academic but still useful (for example, the BBC *Gardeners' World* website is extremely informative for amateur gardeners, yet it wouldn't be a good idea to use it as a sole source to read a plant sciences degree); and the less than useful material.

This book can be read straight off or used as a reference work, something to dip into when the need arises. The text is effectively divided into three parts. Part I is not so much about how to find resources, but rather how to recognise and categorise what it is we do find. We offer a glimpse of the foundations underlying research and of the techniques used to come to grips with the vast array of information on offer (this part comprises Chapters 1 and 2). Our advice would be to familiarise yourself with the terms, tools and discussions in these chapters before reading on and before starting your research.

Before introducing the literature review in Chapter 2 (that is, the one involving books and the like), we start by offering an introduction to the basics of research. The rationale behind such a start is simple. If we are not clear about the language in which research is discussed and disseminated, if we are unclear about the purpose of specific research tools and the meaning of certain research terms, if we have no idea why and how we ought to categorise the information we find, then undertaking the task of producing a coherent essay will be very difficult indeed. In Chapter 1 we briefly touch on such lofty topics as the philosophy of social science, but only in so far as it aids an understanding of what follows and not simply as an exercise in deliberation. Armed with an understanding of the roots of research, you can move on to Chapter 2 and learn the whys and wherefores of the literature review, including techniques for parcelling up the literature into understandable 'chunks'.

Part II, on the other hand, contains the 'what, where and how' behind finding material. There is an emphasis on using web-based sources and how to sort the wheat from the chaff or the good stuff from the potentially useless (Chapters 3–5). Part II opens with a series of chapters dedicated to locating sources. First, we look at tracking down books and articles using the services provided by libraries (Chapter 3) before moving to online resources provided by the same (Chapter 4). The idea is both to show you what resources are available and how to locate them, while keeping in mind a few rules about how to evaluate what it is you do find. Evaluation of resources is a theme throughout, as college and university work is designed to test your ability to sift and select sound sources and not simply amass as much information as possible. Chapter 5 offers advice on navigating the Internet and locating sources without the aid of library services, outlining the advantages and pitfalls of such an approach. We also offer advice on presenting yourself online and discuss the importance of 'netiquette' (online etiquette). The topic of the final chapter (Chapter 6) is referencing and plagiarism and this is probably best read before you even begin the research process. Although it does not sound exciting, this chapter deals with two of the most important areas in academia, as not understanding or respecting the first ('referencing') can often lead to accusations of the second ('plagiarism'). It is crucial to learn the rules and conventions of referencing the literature/sources you locate and use in your work and how to avoid plagiarising, the crime of all crimes in academia (effectively passing off others' work as your own).

Finally, in Part III, at the end of the book, we present an extended glossary of words and concepts related to finding resources. **Concepts** highlighted throughout the book will be listed here and explained more fully. Such a glossary of terms and explanations can be dipped into when needed, either while reading the text or when you need to look up or clarify a specific term.

In order to forefront the notion of evaluation of sources, we have no less than *Six* honest serving men (taken from Kipling, 1940). The six are: 'What', 'Why', 'When', 'How', 'Where' and 'Who', who will keep reminding us to remain vigilant while searching for sources throughout the book.

Part I

Foundations

1 Back to Basics – Understanding and Categorising Research Material

This chapter looks at:
▶ The need to categorise research material
▶ The 'language' of research
▶ The basic foundations of research
▶ Some of the key tools and terms used in research

● Introduction

In everyday life we use all sorts of shortcuts to parcel up and categorise complex social reality. We use words such as 'institutions' or 'women', 'books', 'trust' or 'vehicle'. In general, we know what people are referring to when they use these concepts, but they are very broad and generic. Such concepts tend to act as a necessary 'mental' shorthand to enable us to understand what's going on around us. Without these socially constructed cognitive shortcuts, parcelling the world into understandable, but necessarily oversimplified segments, the world would remain a complex mass of unordered information.

In the social sciences there are many terms relating to attempts to categorise social complexity, ranging from a traditional 'approach' or 'perspective' in an established academic discipline, to a 'paradigm' or school of thought on a specific area of study, for example, health studies, history or international relations. Within each of these particular ways of trying to capture what is going on in the social world there is often a great deal of difference. One of the chief skills of an academic ought to be the ability to present an overview of vast amounts of research, ideas, opinions, approaches, theories and so on, around a certain topic in an understandable and clear fashion. And this is a skill that can and should be learnt by the novice researcher. After all, any successful assignment, essay, report or dissertation will need to draw on a wide range of sources from a variety of authors. What teachers and lecturers do not want to see is a blow-by-blow account of all the sources you have consulted; rather you will need to pick out themes, categorise according to approaches, methods or ideas, in order to present a coherent and clear piece of work (see Chapter 2 for more on categorising literature).

Without any form of classification or categorisation, we would be simply faced with an overwhelming and impenetrable mound of information and facts about our chosen topic.

As we suggest in Chapter 2, without a robust research question or a 'set' essay question – i.e. what it is you are asking/want to find out – to narrow and focus your search for information, it is impossible to begin categorising literature, as some topics (for example, 'democracy' or 'globalisation') have spawned cottage industries of their own, which would take a couple of years to cover.

The techniques used by academics to classify research are many and varied and we will look more closely at them when discussing literature reviews in Chapter 2. In the following examples of classificatory techniques – and these should be looked upon as ways in which to structure a literature review – you should be able to see why spending some time on the research basics is a good idea before beginning research:

- an author's **approach** to a topic (be it 'Marxist' or 'post-modern') can be used as an organising principle with which to categorise literature and research on a specific topic, let's say, the role of the media in society.

Generally, broad 'approaches' in the social sciences can be identified by the questions people ask and how they go about answering them. As we shall see below, this touches on the very foundations upon which research rests and a knowledge of the basics is essential if we have any hope of distinguishing between different ways of undertaking research. Equally, research reviewed could be organised according to:

- the **methodologies** and **methods** used by the authors. Some may draw on a more quantitative research strategy to investigate a particular problem (for example, a content analysis of newspaper output over time); others may make use of in-depth interviews to investigate the same topic (for example, by interviewing those who create the news).

You can, of course, organise reviews on your chosen topic by:

- the arguments put forward: for example, those scholars who suggest that British politics has seen a shift from big 'Government' to a new form of 'governance' by networks, which has resulted in a more democratic and less hierarchical state, and those who argue the opposite: that the proliferation of different government agencies, charities and quangos at different levels has led to a lack of accountability, yet the hierarchy remains (this is a type of 'for' and 'against' argument).

You still need to be aware of how the different scholars arrive at their conclusions; are they asserting this or that or do they actually offer any evidence to back up what they say? There is a distinction between an

- assertion

and an

- argument,

with the former based on little in the way of traceable sources and the latter, if it is good, based on sources that we can track down (Fairbairn and Winch, 2000: 190).

It should be clear by now that any attempt to 'read' the academic or specialist literature in the human and social sciences with any success and with an eye to presenting it clearly requires a knowledge of the key foundational concepts in research (for example, what are 'methods' and 'methodology'?). Many students switch off at this point, feigning other engagements. Whilst we will necessarily dip our toe into the dreaded waters of the philosophy of social science, we will do so only to clarify the roots of research and how these roots affect the rest of the research process.

The 'Language' of Research

Whilst we all know the old cliché, 'knowledge is power', it is worth reflecting on the ways in which knowledge is discussed, disputed and disseminated. In the social sciences there are a number of different 'discourses' between disciplines, for example, economics, history and cultural studies. Common to most discourses is the basic language of research. Given the variety of uses of the terms and terminology of social science research, it is hardly surprising that students rarely have a firm grasp of the tools of their trade. Different academics in different disciplines attach a wide range of meanings and interpretations to the terminology of research. One person's 'theory' is another's 'typology', while another researcher's **ideal type** is another's 'theory', and so on.

With little or no knowledge of the standard reference points in general research, you are likely to produce an essay, dissertation or thesis which is unclear and imprecise: learning the rules of the game simplifies the process, makes it transparent and takes away the fear associated with the unknown. It is our contention that in order to be able to work within the parameters of the social sciences, you need to be very clear about what the tools and terminology of research are and what they mean *before* you can begin researching. If you spend a little time learning the language of research, learning what the terms and concepts mean and how they can be employed, the mystery associated with much of academic work will begin to disappear.

This may sound trivial, but given the fact that many students – and seasoned academics for that matter – have difficulty in differentiating between crucial terms such as

● **ontology** (what is out there to know about in the social world)

and

● **epistemology** (what and how we can know about it),

their subsequent research is bound to suffer, as knowledge of these terms and their place in research is essential to understanding the research process as a whole. These particular terms (ontology and epistemology), for example, are often shrouded in mystery, partly created by the language with which they are explained, leaving readers more confused than they were before they began reading.

What other reasons are there for needing to know and understand standard terms and concepts in social research? A simple example will do: consider a would-be plumber who does not know the difference between a pair of mole grips, a pipe cutter and an olive (not the edible variety). These are some of the basic tools of his trade, without which no tap can be fitted. Each piece of equipment has a specific purpose and, if they are used wrongly (or in the wrong order), for example, attempting to cut a pipe with the mole grips, the results would be disastrous (for budding DIY enthusiasts, mole grips are handy for undoing or doing up compression nuts; pipe cutters do what they say; and olives make taps etc. watertight). In research, specific tools have specific purposes and, if you are to employ them correctly, you must first understand what they mean, what they are meant to do and how and when to use them.

No discussion about the language of research can avoid mentioning the bewildering array of -isms and -ologies used in presenting research. Many of

Use the right tools for the job

these terms are used wrongly or imprecisely by students and academics alike, which adds to the mystery of research and the impenetrability of much of its output. Use of more specific terms, for example, 'variables', 'relation-ships', 'measuring', 'co-variation', 'hypotheses' etc., denotes a sense of seri-ousness, of sound academic judgement, but the fact of the matter is that simply using specific terms is no guarantee of sound research (interestingly, many researchers refuse to use such language as that described above when undertaking and presenting their work, as they do not wish to be associated with a particular research **paradigm**). Students who state boldly in their essays 'Now that I've critically analysed x, y and z ...' after they have done no such thing, do not get extra marks. Saying 'critical analysis' does not equal critical analysis.

● The roots of research

For many students the revelation that there are many different ways of explaining or understanding the same problem is troublesome. Academia is based around this premise. Some academics will explain the collapse of communism in the late 1980s to early 1990s, for example, with an approach that focuses solely on power-wielding elites. This could be labelled a 'top-down approach'. Others may seek to offer an explanation by focusing on economic collapse or the role of citizens in their country's downfall. The latter could be termed a 'bottom-up' approach. Which is correct? What do the authors of these works base their arguments on? Which assumptions underlie their explanations of events? How do we judge between the different approaches? This is the stuff of research. First, we need to acknowledge that there is no 'right' or 'wrong' explanation of the collapse of communism (or whatever your topic is), there are just different takes on it. Additionally, many approaches to the same topic may actually be complementary – for example, power-wielding elites, the deteriorating economy and collective action may well all have contributed to communism's collapse.

For a quick example of how very different perceptions of events and of what constitutes 'reality' can exist, let us turn to Plato's cave analogy. (Note: Plato is regarded as one of the 'greats' of Western philosophy and, of his many texts, the *Republic*, from which this allegory is taken, is still a must-read for anyone interested in understanding key conundrums in the social sciences.) Imagine prisoners in a cave chained in such a way that they can only see forwards, to a wall, upon which shadows of objects, carried by people behind them, are reflected in the light of a fire – so, effectively, they are seeing shadows cast by cut-out shapes of 'real' things (the shape of a lion or a jug, for example). The prisoners then give names and characteristics to the shadows of these objects, which, to them, represent their reality. Plato then imagines a scene in which one prisoner leaves the dark cave and on his way out sees that not only are the shadows cast by objects, but the objects themselves are models of things that exist in reality. In the *Republic*, Plato describes a dialogue between Socrates and Glaucon. Socrates says:

> Suppose someone tells him [the prisoner released from the cave] that what he's been seeing all this time has no substance, and that he's now closer to reality and is seeing more accurately, because of the greater reality of the things in front of his eyes – what do you imagine his reaction would be? And what do you think he'd say if he were shown any of the passing objects and had to respond to being asked what it was? Don't you think he'd be bewildered and would think

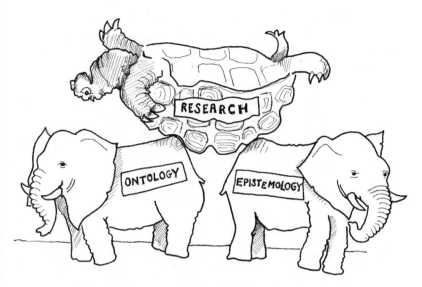

Ontology and epistemology underpin research

> that there was more reality in what he'd been seeing before than in
> what he was being shown now?   (1994: 241–2)

This passage, written over 2000 years ago, offers an insight into the age-old
pre-occupation with how some people can come to think in certain ways,
which are bound by certain cultural and social norms and parameters. Any
premises built upon the experience of the cave dwellers are certain to differ
from those of people who are on the outside. It is for this reason that we
need to understand that *different* views of the world and *different* ways of
gathering knowledge exist. Once we are aware of this, it is easier to begin to
understand and categorise research and to see where our own work fits in,
in relation to it.

● Foundational concepts and their role in the research process: what's your worldview?

This sub-heading may not sound riveting, but without first understanding the
basics of research, we have no hope of trying to sort it out for our own
purposes. Why do you think some authors emphasise in their accounts or
explanations certain aspects of their work over others? For example, if we
adhere to the 'great men [*sic*] make History' approach to understanding the

past, we are focusing on the role of individual actors over the structural contexts in which they act, not to mention the fact that we are forgetting an awful lot of female actors. If we focus on the structures that constrain and shape people's action, we may not leave room for the role of individual actors, their charisma or their ideas. In general, the questions we as researchers pose will be driven and shaped by what are termed our 'ontological and epistemological assumptions' about the world. Stay with us here. They are only words, albeit long and complicated sounding. At their most simple these terms combine to equate to a person's 'worldview', or how that person sees the world, how it is made up. This influences the questions researchers ask, what they believe is important to study and how they go about researching it.

Some examples will illuminate the role a person's worldview plays. We are all individuals, with sometimes very different life experiences, age, gender, upbringing and so on. This make-up will affect the way in which we view society. Social class is one factor – not the only one, of course – which will impact on the way we view the world. If you were a wealthy, white, Oxford-educated man with a formal education in an elite private school ('A'), it is likely that you might have a different view on, say, the role that social class plays in access to elite universities, from that of a poor, white, female educated in a less renowned university ('B'). This is not to suggest that one is better or more worthy than the other: the point is that student 'B' may have worked through her degree, had no support from her family and lived off beans and toast. Student 'A', on a scholarship and stemming from a completely different socio-economic background, is likely to not have had the same experience as student 'B', in particular with reference to food. Thus, if both, after their studies, turned their attention to education and students' access to it, it is probable that they would (a) ask different questions to start with, and (b) use a different approach to answer the questions they posed. It is also possible that they might adopt exactly the same approach, but in general your life experience will shape your ontological position, that is, your views on how the world is made up and what the most important components of the social world are, including such themes as hierarchy (who's in charge of what), patriarchy (the dominant role of men in society), social status and class (Do we live in a classless society? Is there an 'underclass'? Do people from all classes have equal opportunity to access education in elite universities?).

One important point to note, before we get too bogged down in philosophical debates, is that one's ontological position cannot be refuted; that is, no amount of empirical evidence can be brought to bear upon it to prove it wrong. It is akin to a belief system that acts as the foundations of our research.

The worldview of a roast peacock will differ in many ways from that of beans on toast

Why is it important to know that all research necessarily starts from a person's view of the world, which itself is shaped by the experiences they bring to the research process? Well, the manner in which a researcher goes on to undertake research, their choice of approach and research methods, will be influenced by their starting point. When we read articles, books and book chapters, we ought to be looking for the underlying assumptions underpinning the author's argument. Knowledge of this will help us understand the link between the author's starting point, their choice of methodology, and the manner in which they analyse the data they collect.

● Of research 'tools' and 'terms'

One of the problems with learning the basics of research is that the discourse around this topic is confusing and very inconsistent across academic disciplines. What we can do to mitigate against this is to learn the generic meaning of the most basic concepts needed to understand and classify research on our topic. We distinguish between key research 'tools' (those that help us classify) and key research 'terms'. Obviously there are a great number of both, but we will introduce what we consider the most important. All of the 'tools' discussed are used by academics in an attempt to classify, categorise or 'capture' social phenomena (just like our 'mental' shortcuts in the introduction to this chapter). You will almost certainly come across the following in your reading:

- Concept
- Paradigm
- Typology
- Theory

Concepts: explain what you mean

Concepts are the building blocks of any description, explanation or argument; hypotheses and theories are made up of them. Most simply, a concept can be understood as an idea expressed in one or more words. A concept carries with it certain built-in assumptions about the world, or certain ways of understanding empirical phenomena. A concept such as 'athlete', for example, assumes a number of things, including the notion of people competing against one another, physical exercises and games.

In society we tend to agree on the existence of a concept and its broad meaning (for example, a chicken) and this is rarely disputed, but in academic works, agreement does not go far beyond the existence of a concept. The majority of scholars would not deny the existence of the term 'poverty', but discussing what exactly it refers to in the 'real world' or 'on-the-ground' is, in part, what academia is all about and it is rare to have a majority consensus on this. Yet, defining concepts as they are used in research, an essay, a dissertation and so on is probably one of the most important tasks.

Reading an essay or article in which the key concepts are not defined clearly and up-front – let's say, for argument's sake, the concept 'new managerialism' (many concepts claim the prefix 'new') – it is very difficult to assess the work as a whole. What does the author mean by 'managerialism' and what is so new about it anyway? Whose definition are they using; is it an 'official' government definition or has the author invested this concept with specific meaning in the context in which she is writing? It is good practice to set out the meaning of the core concepts you are using in your work as early as is practicable, although, as you shall find out, not all academics follow this rule.

Once a definition has been staked out – this one is very brief so as not to bore you – the reader can assess (a) whether they agree with such a definition, and (b) whether the concept is used consistently and logically throughout the study.

Box 1   Example of defining a concept: 'New Managerialism'

Something along the lines of the following will do for an
undergraduate essay:

> In this work, I [or, 'the author'] characterise 'new managerialism'
> as 'the removal of the locus of power from the knowledge of
> practising professionals to auditors, policy-makers and
> statisticians' (Davies, 2003: 91), who do not need to have an
> intimate knowledge of the area in which they are working. In brief,
> the concept 'new managerialism' is short-hand for a process well
> underway in many British public institutions and government
> departments in which a one-size-fits-all model based on business
> practice has been rolled out to 'modernise' their governance (for a
> full example, see Grix, 2009: 33–5).

Paradigm

What a nice word; however, it is often misused, confused and put in place of
all sorts of other classificatory terms, by academics and students alike, for
example: model, perspective, approach or typology. The common use, in
research, of the term 'paradigm' draws directly on Thomas Kuhn, who
depicts a paradigm as an institutionalisation of intellectual activity which, in
effect, socialises students into their respective scientific community. Kuhn
explains:

> By choosing [the term 'paradigm'], I mean to suggest that some
> accepted examples of actual scientific practice – examples which
> include law, theory, application, and instrumentation together –
> provide models from which spring particular coherent traditions of
> scientific research. ... The study of paradigms ... is what mainly
> prepares the student for membership in the particular scientific
> community with which he will later practice. Because he there joins
> men who learned the bases of their field from the same concrete
> models, his subsequent practice will seldom evoke overt disagree-
> ment over fundamentals.   (1996: 10–11)

In the social sciences, the term has come to mean, or is not dissimilar to, 'an
established academic approach'. Furthermore, paradigms are often overtaken, replaced or placed alongside other paradigms, leading to what is
commonly called a 'paradigm shift'.

Box 2   Examples of a 'paradigm' shift

In German diasporic literature written between the 1970s and 1990s, the 'two worlds paradigm' was the dominant approach to depicting a migrant's view of their world. Characters in such literature make frequent references to having fallen between two stools, or to being trapped between two opposing worlds.

However, in German diasporic literature written from the late 1990s onwards, the 'two worlds paradigm' is referred to far less frequently. This paradigm is now considered outdated, and it is something which writers of modern diasporic literature rarely seem to draw upon in their work.

Some critics even believe that relying on this paradigm hampers our enjoyment and understanding of diasporic literature. This paradigm has now shifted almost entirely.

In macro-economics the neoclassical paradigm (or 'school of thought') and its worldview has, since the late 1960s/early 1970s, taken over as the dominant approach from its predecessor, Keynesianism. Both of these paradigms are based on specific ontological and epistemological assumptions which are reflected in the emphasis and priority they place on specific factors, although there is, of course, limited variation on these matters within both paradigms among protagonists. Whilst neo-classical economists advocate the virtues of an unfettered market and a small role for the state, Keynesian approaches usually call for a more active role of the state in stimulating the economy. The dominance of the neo-classical economics approach has taken a severe bashing because of the so-called 'credit crunch' and perhaps another, altered way of managing the economy will emerge in years to come.

However, whilst 'dominant' paradigms exist and are often challenged in the human and social sciences, we are not talking about the same kind of 'paradigms' that dominate in the natural sciences.

The use of paradigms in everyday research, however, should be limited to crude and broad groupings of certain approaches to the study of a specific topic – for example, you may separate out those approaches to your topic which focus on structural explanations of an event and those that focus more on agents (see Chapter 2 for more on categorising literature).

Box 3   What's in a paradigm?

You need to differentiate between the following three concepts:

paradigm: this should be reserved for broad definitions, for example, the 'positivist' paradigm of research (within which there will be vast differences between proponents);

discipline: this usually applies to 'traditional' academic disciplines like economics, history, political science etc. (disciplines also contain a multitude of sub-disciplines and are not paradigms themselves);

perspective: an academic perspective pertains to (a) certain approaches *within* a discipline, for example, new institutionalism and rational choice in political science, and (b) approaches that transcend narrow academic disciplines, for example, a feminist or post-modern perspective.

This is a general method of broad categorisation of roughly related approaches to specific phenomena – it has little to do with the Kuhnian sense of 'paradigm' in the natural sciences. What it does do is to allow you to focus and structure your observations, otherwise you will end up writing an interesting story without being able to begin to differentiate, at least, between the ways in which people approach a specific topic.

The term 'paradigm' is, however, good for describing broad approaches to research, for example, the '**positivist**' or '**interpretivist**' paradigms, within which many academic perspectives draw from similar ontological and epistemological roots (for an overview of research paradigms, see Grix, 2010).

Typologies: bringing some order out of chaos

Typologies are similar systems of classification to ideal types. They can generally be seen as loose frameworks with which to organise and systematise our observations. Typologies do not provide us with explanations, rather they describe empirical phenomena – in other words, what's going on in the 'real' world – by fitting them into a set of categories. What they do help researchers with is the organisation of a wide range of diverse facts that can be structured into logical, but sometimes arbitrary, categories, which helps us in getting a grip of what is happening around us.

Take, for example, Gospa Esping-Andersen's often cited three-fold typology of welfare regimes. Remember, with the following we are grossly oversimplifying what is already an oversimplification of reality for the purpose of getting across our point on the need for categories in life in general and research in particular. Esping-Andersen came up with three broad typologies to describe different types of European welfare states (these truncated versions are for demonstration purpose only; for an accurate representation of these typologies, please read the original, in Esping-Andersen 1990; abridged from Hodgson and Irving, 2007: 38–9):

Social democratic (in this category social policy maximises the capacity for individual independence; women are encouraged to participate in employment – for example, Austria and Belgium);

Liberal (these states strongly encourage individualism and self-reliance; the state intervenes but only to support the market; women are encouraged to participate in employment – for example, the UK);

Conservative (a bit of a mixture of the above; however, women are not encouraged to participate in the labour market – for example, Germany and Italy).

Box 4   Typology example

Formally speaking, the construction of typologies is the attempt to develop a single variable through the interaction of two or more further variables. And this is exactly what Aristotle did in his attempt to classify regime types.

By taking the 'form' of rule (either 'good' or 'corrupt') (variable 1)

and factoring in the different number of rulers making up the decision-making body (either 'one', 'few' or 'many') (variable 2),

Aristotle came up with six different types of regime (variable 3): monarchy, aristocracy and polity (the 'good' regime types) and tyranny, oligarchy and democracy (the 'corrupt' regime types).

Aristotle's conclusion is that the best form of rule is a mixture of oligarchy and democracy to make 'polity', that is, a form of rule led by the 'middle people' (neither the rich, nor the poor) (Aristotle, 1948: 261–72; also see Haywood, 2002, for further explanation).

The point is that Aristotle categorised forms of rule first, he then put them in groups, noting their characteristics, and finally, used comparison to come up with a preferred way to govern.

The point here is not to get carried away with the detail – what these typologies do is to 'bring order out of chaos'. If you study individual welfare regimes they are a complex web of history, politics, political culture, social policy and economics.

Countries as diverse as Switzerland, Sweden and the UK may well have very different welfare regimes, aims and historical trajectories. What these broad categories do is begin to sort them into roughly cognate systems for comparison. Built on the earliest classification scheme proposed by Aristotle (see Box 4 above), the typology serves to 'reduce the complexity of the world by seeking out those qualities that countries (or cases) share and those that they do not share' (Landman, 2000: 5).

Theory: seeking clarity

Now, if concepts are fairly easy to grasp, paradigms can be learnt, and it is fairly clear how typologies can be used in research, **theory** is a different kettle of fish. There are a number of problems with attempting to define 'theory' and they are not due to theory being complex or incomprehensible, as, perhaps counter-intuitively, the best theories are often the most simple to understand and employ – in fact, before we start it may be a good idea to state the purpose of theory: it is not to baffle your readers, leaving them floundering in a cloak of terminological mist; losing them with impenetrable prose that only a select few could possibly understand. No, the purpose of theory or any theoretical framework is the opposite to bafflement: it is actually to *simplify* complex social reality in order to explain or understand it. This is often unfortunately forgotten, especially in undergraduate essays. Now, one of the problems in defining 'theory' lies in the fact that *all* research is theoretical, even that which claims not to be. As we set out above, anything we study and write on will be influenced by our own worldview and this is what is sometimes grandly termed the 'meta-theoretical' level. Basically this refers to the foundational elements of research touched on above and can be looked upon as the most abstract of all theory. This leads to the next problem of definition: there are several different types of theory (for example, middle-range, grounded and grand theory). To make things worse, researchers working in different research paradigms – see above – have different ideas about what theory is and what its role is in research. Suffice to say, it is best to learn and familiarise yourselves with the different types and uses of theory (see the Glossary under '**theory**') so you can read academic literature with a degree of confidence. Here are just some you are bound to come across:

- Meta-theory
- Grand theory

- Middle-range theory
- **Grounded theory**

Whatever they are called, most theories have one thing in common: they attempt to simplify complex social phenomena. Their general purpose – although the finer points of this are hotly disputed among academics – is to shed light on and make sense of what's going on in the social world. Some academics believe in the ability of theories to predict; others see them as ways of explaining relationships between concepts, for example, athletics training and fitness levels. In the social sciences we do not enjoy the clearer links between factors that natural or medical scientists do. Generally, it has come to be understood that smoking is not at all good for you and in fact you are far more likely to develop cancer as a result. Finding such '**causal**' links (that is: 'smoking' can cause 'cancer') in the social world is fraught with difficulties, not least because we cannot undertake lab-like experiments, in which many other factors ('variables') are held constant.

Methods and methodology

Methods

At the root of all research lies what the ancient Greeks termed *methodos*. On the one hand, the term means 'the path towards knowledge', and on the other, 'reflections on the quest for knowledge-gathering'. Many of the central concerns of research have their roots firmly in the work of ancient Greek philosophers. Witness, for example, the manner in which Socrates, Plato and Aristotle employed classificatory systems or typologies of states, types of rule, etc., to make sense of the social phenomena surrounding them.

We follow Norman Blaikie's (2000) more modern definition of **methods** and **methodology**, two words that are often confused, used interchangeably and generally misunderstood. The former is easier to explain and understand than the latter. Research methods, quite simply, can be seen as the 'techniques or procedures used to collate and analyse data' (Blaikie, 2000: 8). The method(s) chosen for a research project are inextricably linked to the **research questions** posed and to the **sources** of data collected.

Research methods come in all shapes and sizes, ranging from in-depth interviews, statistical inference, discourse analysis and archival research of historical documents, to participant observation. The choice of methods will be influenced by your worldview (made up of those dreaded ontological and epistemological assumptions), which affects the questions you are asking, and by the *type* of project you are undertaking, e.g. either researching individuals' attitudes or institutional change.

Within the academic community, some methods are looked upon and associated with 'good research', whilst others are not. Remember that good scholarship is not just the result of a specific method, but the result of *how* you employ, cross-check, collate and analyse the data that methods assist you in collecting. Your work should be judged on how its constituent parts logically link together, not by which methods you use.

Box 5   The link between a research question (RQ), methods and sources

Let's say we are interested in the image of Germany in the UK media. We want to research the manner in which Germany and the Germans are reported about. Most commentators agree that the media present a stereotypical view of Germany, but not much research actually exists to show this. We can turn this into a RQ: 'How is Germany (and the Germans) represented in the UK print media?' Or 'Is the coverage of Germany and the Germans in UK print media stereotypical?'

Now, our RQ will lead us to the research methods and research sources that will answer our question. First, we need to narrow our study down to specific media, for example, newspapers. We can then choose a specific time period (otherwise the project will be much too big), then set about gathering articles covering Germany and the Germans. Our RQ has led us to the method of document analysis (of newspapers in this case) and the sources are the articles themselves. Depending on the size and level of the project, we may want to speak to actors who work in British–German relations, using the interview technique. Thus, our original question has led us to:

- Newspaper articles (sources)
- Documentary analysis (research method)
- Interview technique (research method)
- Interview transcripts (raw data derived from interviews)

Therefore a RQ should lead to our method (M) and our sources (RQ → M → S).

What you ought to avoid is 'method-led' research, whereby the focus of the project is led by methods and not the research question (see Grix and Lacroix, 2006, from which this example of Germany is taken).

An advanced undergraduate essay, dissertation or doctoral thesis without any method, however loosely defined, is an out-and-out contradiction. In research, methods have two principal functions:

- they offer the researcher a way of gathering information or gaining insight into a particular issue;
- they enable another researcher to re-enact the first's endeavours by emulating the methods employed.

Methods can be used in either

- **quantitative research**, which is concerned predominantly with quantity and quantifying, or
- **qualitative research**, which is concerned with interpreting the subjective experiences, i.e. the perspectives, of the individuals being studied.

Methodology

Now for the slightly trickier definition. Methodology is concerned with the logic of scientific enquiry; in particular with investigating the potentialities and limitations of particular techniques or procedures. The term pertains to the science and study of methods and the assumptions about the ways in which knowledge is produced. The difficulty in understanding just what the term 'methodology' means has not been helped by the fact that it is used interchangeably with 'research methods' and is often considered, mistakenly, to be close in meaning to 'epistemology', 'approaches', and even 'paradigm'. 'Epistemology' should be looked upon as an overarching philosophical term concerned with the origin, nature and limits of human knowledge, and the knowledge-gathering process itself. A project's methodology, on the other hand, is concerned with the discussion of how a particular piece of research should be undertaken, and can be understood as the critical study of research methods and their use. This term refers to the *choice* of research strategy taken by a particular scholar – as opposed to other, alternative research strategies.

The methodology section of a project, undergraduate dissertation, Master's or doctoral thesis, which is, especially in political science, often replaced with a section on 'ontology and epistemology', has come to mean 'the difficult bit' among students, through which they have to wade before being allowed to go off 'in the field' and enjoy themselves. A student's methodology is driven by a certain worldview and consists of research questions or hypotheses, a conceptual approach to a topic, the methods to be used in the study – and their justification – and, consequently, the data sources.

All of these components are inextricably linked to one another in a logical manner. This is also the section that can take the most time, as students attempt to place their work among the canon of existing works on their topic, drawing on insights from wide-ranging literature reviews, and developing an 'innovative' angle on events. The extent to which this is done will depend on the level at which the student is studying. For an essay at an FE (Further Education) college the criteria are likely to be different from those of a final year undergraduate student at university (for advice on the extent of literature reviews, see Chapter 2). As a general rule, the longer the piece of work (an undergraduate dissertation, a Master's and so on), the greater the emphasis on the methodology section.

Summary

☐ Categorisation and classification are essential to everyday life. Academics spend a great deal of their time categorising and attempting to bring order to the study of what is, effectively, a 'messy' subject: the social world.

☐ To understand the process of categorisation, the tools used and terms employed, we must first learn the 'language' of research. Unfortunately, much discussion around the foundations of research and the tools used in research is enveloped in a dense fog of impenetrable prose.

☐ This chapter attempted to introduce the basics of research necessary for starting your search for information and lifting this dense fog.

Jargon buster

Learn the following from this chapter:

- Concept
- Typology
- Paradigm
- Theory
- Ontology
- Epistemology
- Methodology
- Methods

2 The Literature Review

● What is a literature review?

The obvious answer to this question is a 'review of the literature', but this does not get us very far. The first thing to note is the distinction between a 'literature search' – not a 'literary search' as some students grandly suggest – and a 'literature review'. The 'search' generally refers to the process of tracking down and getting your hands on the actual literature to read; the 'review' generally consists of an analysis of the material gathered. In what follows, we use the term 'literature review' to cover both these processes. Bear in mind too that 'literature' does not simply mean 'books' and 'articles', for, as we shall see, literature comes in many shapes and sizes, including newspapers, CDs and DVDs, and past dissertations.

The question to discuss initially is 'why do we have to review the literature in the first place?' The answer to this will vary depending on what level you are working at: an 'A' level student (the UK equivalent of university entry-level) would need to worry far less about their literature review than would a doctoral student studying for a PhD (Philosophiae Doctor; Doctor of Philosophy), given that the very purpose of the latter is an original contribution to knowledge. Although there are great differences between levels of study, and the size of the review and amount of literature to be consulted, many principles remain the same. For example, relying heavily on single sources of information (such as using one particular book or article) is never a good idea whatever the level you are working at, as there are many different ways of understanding or interpreting the same thing, be it an event, crises, war and so on. Also, simply taking one person's ideas and regurgitating them is hardly research. A good essay weighs up the strengths and weaknesses of a variety of approaches, in the process necessarily covering more than one opinion.

Box 6   Don't forget the library!

Many students, brought up on a diet of information technology, fail to see the benefit of actually going to the library and picking a book from the shelf. We believe that such a process aids the construction of an argument, teaches reflection on the part of students and is an essential complement to on-line resource retrieval (dealt with in Chapters 3–5). The process of actually tracking down, finding and reading a 'traditional' source can be seen as a check against the ever faster desk-bound studies students are copying and pasting together using multiple web-based sources. The actual process of obtaining literature for academic work is becoming increasingly easier (there is hardly any need to get out of your chair to locate a good journal article, formerly a time-consuming process); however, there is much more information to choose from than in the past (as you'll see in Chapters 3–5 on locating web-based sources).

● The role of the literature review in research, essays and dissertations

The literature review is perhaps the best known, yet least understood method of starting a project, be it an essay, MA or work report. Reviewing the secondary literature on a given topic area is common to all of these, whether in the social sciences, humanities or place of work. In academic work, the first thing to note is that reviewing the literature is not a compartmentalised stage of research. Instead, the student and scholar *constantly* reviews the literature until the day their project is submitted, by which time the last thing they want to hear about is a newly published study on exactly their topic. The review serves many purposes and is undertaken in many stages. However, common to all (from essays to PhDs), is that the review gives context to the work that follows, allows the reader to understand the broader issues at stake, offers a chance of finding out what has or what has not been written on a given topic and provides the student with the opportunity to indicate where her work 'fits' with the existing literature around the chosen topic and why it is worth undertaking the project in light of this.

We suggest that there is a continuum which begins at one end with the initial 'dip' into the academic literature and ends, in the period shortly prior to submitting your work, with a 'checking' or 'skimming' of the literature. These two extremes represent two different reasons for reviewing the literature. As you move along the continuum from the initial literature review to the 'skimming' stage, the purpose of the ongoing review changes. These broad stages are discussed further below.

Apart from getting you started on your research project, Table 2.1 outlines other reasons for reviewing the literature. You will see how the 'rationale' for a literature review depends on what it is you are writing.

Rationale	Important for:
Acquaint you with the sum of the accumulated knowledge and understanding in a given field and around a particular question or topic, otherwise known as the 'cutting edge' of research	Most essential for postgraduate students
Expose you to, and enable you to demonstrate a familiarity with, the approaches, theories, methods and sources used in your topic area	This is usually a prerequisite of a PhD thesis and a key theme of the **viva** to which examiners will turn; also important for an MA, final year undergraduate dissertation, and undergraduate essays in general
Assist you in identifying a 'gap' in this literature, thereby justifying your particular study's contribution to research, and assisting in your choice of approach and methods	Mostly for advanced undergraduates and postgraduates; although you can show 'gaps' or areas that need more research in essays/undergraduate essays
Highlight the key debates, terms and concepts employed in your topic area	For most: you will need to make reference to these in your 'review'
Contextualise your project within a wide-ranging existing knowledge base	All need to show the context in which they, and the debates therein, are set
See what has been written on your topic already	For all essays, dissertations etc.
Focus and clarify your research problem or your 'take' on the chosen topic	For all essays, dissertations etc.

Table 2.1   Reasons for reviewing the literature

In a literature review you must, above all, make reference to, and engage with, the key texts in your chosen field or on and around your topic (by 'engaging' we mean you weigh up ideas, look for strengths and weaknesses etc., and not simply repeat what someone has written). Before you can do this, however, you need to know *where* to look for the literature to review (this is the 'search' bit). There is a vast number of places to find literature, including the standard academic sources such as:

- library catalogues, indexes and **abstracts**;
- dissertations and theses (a university library, for example, usually stores one copy of all doctoral theses produced – and passed successfully – at their institution, which offers a great source of information for students);
- back issues of relevant scholarly journals (both 'hard copies' and web-based);
- CDs and DVDs;
- specific documentation centres (these may be subject specific, political or geographical, for example, the 'German Studies Documentation Centre').

Chapters 3 and 4 will show you how to find, cite and evaluate web-based sources.

● Everything comes in threes

Three approximate stages of the ongoing literature review can be summed up thus: the initial 'dip' (literature review I), the 'research question or hypothesis' stage (literature review II), and 'the critical review' stage (literature review III). In between all of these stages, you must find time actually to read whole articles or books, as students under any type of pressure (be it temporal or financial) naturally try to cut corners. An additional type of literature review is the so-called 'skimming' technique, which you can only really undertake once you are already very familiar with a topic and have grasped the core assumptions, arguments and debates contained therein. Before we introduce the three 'stages' of a literature review, Table 2.2 gives you a rough guide on what you should be aiming for at different levels of work. The three types of literature review are listed, along with a column indicating the minimum number of sources required for specific levels of work – these sources are 'traditional' and should be in addition to web-based sources. For example, for a standard third-year undergraduate university essay in the

The Literature Review 31

	Literature review (I)	Literature review (II)	Literature review (III)	Number of sources needed	Current state of knowledge	Contribution to knowledge
College essay	✓	(✓)				
University essay: 1st year; 3rd year	1st/3rd	1st, 2nd/3rd	3rd	1st = min. of 6; 2nd = min. of 8; 3rd = min. of 10*	3rd Should indicate key debates	No
3rd year university dissertation	✓	✓	✓	Minimum of 15*	Should indicate key debates	No
MA dissertation	✓	✓	✓	✓	Minimum of 20–25* Should indicate key debates	Can contribute, but not a prerequisite
PhD thesis	✓	✓	✓	50+*	Ought to outline the current state of knowledge	Need to indicate how work will advance current knowledge

Table 2.2 What to aim for at different levels of work

* These figures are the *minimum* number of sources recommended.

social sciences one would expect a source-base of at least 10 books or articles. The number 10 in this example does not include 6 entries for Wikipedia references or other web-based material (the exception being, of course, journal articles and bona fide documents, for example, downloadable government department policy papers). The numbers of sources given are indicative only and based on our own experience and good practice – check with your own institution at the start of the modules you are studying. A final two columns are added entitled 'Current state of knowledge' and 'Contribution to knowledge' to show you what is expected of higher degrees.

The initial 'dip' (literature review I)

At the very start of a project, *any* project, the best thing to do is to undertake an initial review of the relevant literature. This might be guided by the 'hunches' you have already, by sheer interest in a topic or by the tutor's list of essay question topics. During this stage, your initial 'gut' feelings will be quite quickly confirmed or corrected, which will assist you in gradually acquiring knowledge of your subject, and, more importantly, if it is done correctly, it will give you a broad overview of what has been written already. Let us take the example of 'drugs in sport'. Intuitively, we might think that most literature on this would come out strongly against the use of performance-enhancing drugs in sport, as it goes against the very principles of fair play. An initial 'dip' in the literature will reveal a surprising find: many authors actually argue against a ban on drugs (this is not because they believe in using drugs, but rather, they feel that it is futile to attempt to police their use). This makes an essay on this topic easier, because we already have a neat division of those who are 'for' and those who are 'against', just one way we can divide up the literature and position our own view point (to support a ban on drugs, for the sake of argument). We will return to this example below.

There is no point in setting a specific time limit for the 'dip' stage of the review, because everyone works at different speeds and has differential access to material. Suffice it to say, if you are undertaking a longer piece of work, you ought to agree with your tutor or supervisor on a set period of time to undertake this stage. If you are writing one of many essays, you will need to be much snappier. Of course, the time you need to spend on this stage will differ, depending on the level at which you are studying.

Quasimodo says: 'Rely on your hunch and "information skills"'

Box 7 Advice for the budding postgraduate

We would recommend for an MA, four weeks, for a PhD, six to eight weeks of uninterrupted searching and reading, which should be sufficient for you to obtain an *overview* of the relevant literature in your field. A good idea is to ask an experienced academic who works in your field for some tips regarding literature. After consulting your supervisor, you could even seek advice by email from someone you do not know personally, as some are happy to help research students, especially those who are copiously citing their work. Academics' addresses, emails, and so on can usually be found in your relevant association's directory – for example, the *American Political Science Association Directory* or the *Political Science Association/British International Studies Association Directory* has contact details of people in politics and international relations in the US and UK (the same principle applies to most disciplines – sociology, geography, health, social work, history etc. – simply locate your key association, consider joining it – it usually brings benefits – or visit the association's website). Or, if you know someone's academic affiliation, it is usually easy to find their email address from their university's website. Try to get them to guide you to the key texts or articles, including their own work, that you should read. What are, generally speaking, the key debates and approaches to the subject in your field? One of the key tasks of postgraduate work is to 'make an intervention in the literature' on a specific topic, so effectively finding a gap and attempting to plug it.

Once you have located, photocopied or obtained the key literature around your topic, you can set about reading it. (The act of 'reading' is another important factor in the literature review. Some students, believe it or not, read too much, or worse still, do not stick to the material that is relevant. Reading too much is not a problem generally encountered, however, as reading too little is still the major cause of low marks for essays. See below for some tips on 'reading'.) You should, even at this early stage, attempt to begin to roughly organise and categorise the literature (this is a technique for understanding and structuring your review). This can be done in a number of ways, ranging from the 'approach' an author is taking, to the type of sources they are drawing upon. In our 'drugs in sport' example, a simple organising principle could be along the lines of 'for' and 'against', in which we would lump together all those authors who support a ban on drugs in sport and all those who want to see them legalised. While this is good for an essay, we may want to refine the division a little more for a longer piece of work: some authors we have grouped together may draw from very different 'research paradigms' (see the Glossary for more on 'research paradigms' and 'approaches' to research); some may use very different methods and sources to arrive at their conclusions. Table 2.3 gives some examples of how you can begin to parcel and categorise literature as a way of structuring the review. Remember: the idea is to get a handle on the literature around a specific topic and some of the divisions will appear 'artificial'. This is fine and exactly what academics do in their articles all the time: they attempt to categorise and make sense of complicated social phenomena.

The point is that you need some way of categorising the literature you are collecting, in order for you to be able to present a logical review within which you can 'place' what it is you are attempting to argue. If you are not arguing anything, you don't have an essay, even at 'A' level. The 'literature review I' is probably enough for an 'A' level and college level essay, but not for more extended projects. Once you have read, digested and attempted an

Example	Explanation
Broad 'paradigms'	For example, 'top-down' or 'bottom-up' explanations for the collapse of communism. The former concentrate on power-wielding elites (Gorbachev etc.), the latter focus on the actions of ordinary people and ordinary lives (the 'masses'). For a real-world example on this topic, see Grix (1998).
Research 'paradigms'	Basically, researchers using the same starting point, drawing from the same view of the world, employing the same methods could be grouped together, for example, 'interpretivists' or 'positivists'. This division requires knowledge of the foundations of research and is more essential for advanced undergraduates and postgraduates (see Glossary under '**paradigm**'). For an example of using the research paradigms to divide up literature on 'social capital', see Grix (2001).
'Natural' divisions	Take, for example, the 'for' and 'against' scenario in the 'drugs in sport' debate; there may be explanations based on 'external' or 'internal' factors; authors may focus on, or emphasise, specific actors in history (e.g., Margaret Thatcher) or specific structural aspects (institutional change), and so on.

Table 2.3   Suggested categories for structuring reviews

initial categorisation of the literature you have collected, you are ready to move on to the next stage in the review and in the research process: generating research questions. Or, if you have a 'set' question, it is now time to approach the literature more carefully with this specific question in mind.

Research question(s) (literature review II)

Before embarking on a full-scale search of everything that has ever been written on your topic, you need to find a way of narrowing your focus. If you have been set a question, then obviously use this; if not, the best way to focus is to go through a process of developing 'hunches' or ideas into research questions and/or hypotheses to guide your work. There is no agreed way of arriving at a research question or hypothesis, but most researchers are convinced you do need one to begin the research process. Your own interest, ideas, previous research and personal experience will have led you to the field on which you wish to concentrate. (Interestingly, in our experience it has become increasingly hard for students to come up with

Rhino Poo

Narrow your focus, don't restrict it

their own research question. It is a skill in itself: for obvious reasons, you should avoid asking questions that can be answered with either 'yes' or 'no'.) The initial literature review would have assisted you in selecting a broad topic for study within that field. Now you are ready to set out a research question or *proposition* about your chosen area of study. There is a tension here between those scholars who would suggest that it is too early to narrow your focus, and those who believe that, given the time constraints most students are up against, you need to narrow your focus relatively early. Do be aware that proceeding this way does not imply that you must *restrict* your overall research focus, for you can adapt and firm up your questions and propositions later in the research process.

Let us take another broad research question as an example. Let's say our area of interest is 'Shakespeare's use of doubt and certainty'. Within this huge field of study, we are specifically interested in Shakespeare's use of doubt and certainty in his tragedies. To guide our research initially – and to guide our reading – we could pose the following question: 'How does Shakespeare explore the contrasting notions of doubt and certainty in his tragedies?' You can't answer 'yes' or 'no' to this, as the 'how' implies the need for some explanation.

From the literature on Shakespeare's use of doubt and certainty in his tragedies we would have read about a whole range of theories and approaches to answering this question. We may therefore wish to narrow our focus to, say, Shakespeare's use of doubt and certainty in two of his tragic plays: *King Lear* and *Richard II*. For our research question, we could refine it a little from the simple research question above to 'How does Shakespeare explore the notions of doubt and certainty in *King Lear* and

Richard II?' We would already know from our dip into literature that there are countless articles and books that have been written about this topic, so armed with this more refined research question, we would be able to move on to 'literature review II'.

Let us look at another broad research question as an example. Let's say our area of interest is 'sport and politics'. Here, we are specifically interested in the investment by governments in elite sport. To guide our initial research and our reading, we could pose the following question: 'Why do governments invest in elite sport?' You can't answer 'yes' or 'no' to this either, as the 'why' implies the need for some explanation. You need to decide whether you wish to use a research question to guide your work or a more abstract tool, a hypothesis. Do not insist on using hypotheses when a specific research question would do. Both of these tools will assist the research process by guiding your reading in a full-scale literature review, and by helping you select methods and particular sources. It is very important at this stage to decide how you will formulate your research problem, as this will shape the rest of the research process.

> ### Box 8 What's a hypothesis?
>
> A hypothesis states a relationship between two, or more, concepts and suggests that one has an impact on the other. Verma and Beard sum up a hypothesis and its role in research as:
>
> > A tentative proposition which is subject to verification through subsequent investigation, it may also be seen as the guide to the researcher in that it depicts and describes the method to be followed in studying the problem. In many cases hypotheses are hunches that the researcher has about the existence of relationship between variables (1981: 184, cited in Bell, 1993: 18).

A hypothesis is different from a research question in as much as it is usually more closely linked to a theory, and will posit the answer to a research question within itself which will subsequently be 'tested' in field-work. The choice of which to use in a study will be governed by the type of study you wish to undertake; for example, it is fair to say that a straightforward and clear research question will suffice for most studies. The research question above could be formulated in a hypothesis, if this were appropriate (see Boxes 8 and 9 for what a hypothesis is and how to set one out). From the literature on the involvement of governments in sport we would have read about both democratic and non-democratic (totalitarian, fascist and so on) government intervention in sport. We may wish to narrow our focus to, say, the UK Government and the reasons why it has recently invested so much into elite sport. For our research question, we could refine it a little from the simple research question above to: 'Why does the UK government invest in elite sport?' ('elite sport' generally refers to performance sport; sport at the highest level). We would already know from our 'dip' in the literature that current investment levels are unprecedented (and have been increasing year on year since the 1990s) and are not only due to the London Olympics in 2012. Armed with this slightly more refined research question, and keeping our refined question or our set question at the forefront of out minds, we are ready to move on to 'literature review II'.

Box 9   To hypothesise or not

You may wish to use a hypothesis to drive your essay/dissertation etc. Well, the concepts in the hypothesis need to be *measured* in some way so that it can be 'tested'. To convert concepts into measures, often called the 'operationalisation' of concepts in research, the researcher develops variables, which can be understood, simply, as concepts that vary in amount or kind. Using the same example as our research question, you could set it out like this:

This simplified hypothesis states that there is a positive relationship, indicated by the plus sign, between the concepts 'government investment in elite sport' and 'international prestige, feel-good factor'. In this uncomplicated example, the box labelled 'Government investment in elite sport' is sometimes referred to as the **independent variable** (shown as 'X' in formal models; also depicted as 'IV'). It is also known as 'a causal variable, an explanatory variable, an exogenous variable, or the explicandum' (Landman, 2000: 17), or the thing that 'causes' something else – in this example, change in international prestige and the development of a feel-good factor. The latter, sometimes depicted as 'Y' or 'DV' in formal models, is termed the **dependent variable**. Other terms for this include 'outcome variables, endogenous variables, or the explanandum' (ibid., p. 16), or simply the thing which is 'caused' by the independent variable. It is important to be aware that every dependent variable can be an independent variable, or vice versa: it is the *researcher* who decides where to place the emphasis. Obviously, you would need to clarify just what it is you mean by the concepts you are using. For example, how can we recognise 'international prestige' through sport when we see it? How do I detect a 'feel-good' factor and how does it differ from a 'feel-bad' factor? Interestingly, these are questions not answered by the Labour-led British Government, which posits the hypothetical relationship between elite sport and these factors in its sports policy statements (see Department for Culture, Media and Sport, 2002).

The 'literature review II' would result in unpacking the following debates, strands of research and sources around the theme of government involvement in sport:

- general (generic) studies on sport and politics;
- general (generic) studies on elite sport (and sport models), as opposed to, say, school or community sport;
- (generic) academic works concerning government involvement in elite sport (i.e. the 'wider' debates on why any government invests in elite sport, ranging from sport in the Cold War, to a wide variety of leading sport models, including East Germany, Australia, Canada, the US etc.);
- the arguments put forward explaining government investment in elite sport, including:

  - international prestige, 'feel-good' factor among citizens, and legitimacy,
  - to encourage and inspire the 'masses' to take up sport,
  - economic reasons associated with elite success;

- a wealth of UK government sports policy documents explaining the various reasons behind the investment in elite sport;
- the variety of disciplinary approaches to this topic, ranging from sociology, to sports studies, to political science and area studies;
- also material on what is a democratic and non-democratic government; what is elite sport (and how it is distinguished from 'mass', 'community' and 'school' sport – this could be termed 'generic classificatory' literature);
- you will also need something on the 'method' of your research (say, for example, a form of document analysis).

From this breakdown of literature around our example, we can see there is a lot of material on the topic and on how we define and undertake our research. There is nothing worse than launching into an essay expecting the reader to know what a 'totalitarian' regime is or what 'democracy' means. You need to define the term's use in your essay. It is best to assume the reader – usually a tutor – is ignorant of these facts and so you need to clarify your terms precisely.

We should now try to refine our research question further and narrow our focus, moving as we do from the general (over-arching reasons for government investment in elite sport) to the particular (the reasons why the UK government, in particular, invests in elite sport). Let's say we opt for the argument that the UK government spends so much on elite sport in the hope of obtaining 'international prestige' and a 'feel-good' factor among the population through elite sport success. Please note that these examples have not been added for comic effect – they represent actual examples from Labour Government sport policy documents; see the Department for Culture, Media and Sport, *Game Plan*, 2002, if you don't believe us. We can now reformulate our question. This could be done in several ways, but based on the 'literature review II' we could suggest: 'Can success in elite

Research question: is it possible to 'feel good' at a curling match?

sport bring the UK "international prestige" and generate a "feel-good" factor among its citizens?' We also need to think about a time period for our study: are we concentrating on the last decade? Are there any 'natural' breaks, for example, 1997, when the Labour Party came to power in Britain? What about specific 'case studies'? Should we focus on a few sports more in-depth or discuss elite sport as a whole? Why, for example, does the government invest more in athletics than, say, curling?

We have moved from the very broad question of 'government investment in elite sport' to a case study of the reasons why the UK government, and the Labour government (between 1997 and 2009), believe they should invest in elite sport ('international prestige' and a 'feel-good' factor among citizens). This we can now critically assess against the literature, in our final review.

Full-scale critical literature review (III)

After revising our research question, we are ready to undertake a thorough review of the literature, which will enable us to:

- become further acquainted with the literature around government involvement in sport, including the classic historical examples of the Nazi Olympics, the East German, Russian and Chinese sport systems;
- gain insight into the key debates and major reasons behind government intervention and investment in elite sport (usually for reasons of international legitimacy or prestige);
- learn how other, more experienced researchers analyse the subject and which theories, methods and sources they employ (there are not too many scholars asking this question of 'why' we invest in elite sport; methods would generally involve a form of critical documentary analysis; sources include government documents and archival material for historical cases);
- sharpen and narrow our focus of enquiry further to particular sports as case studies (a good idea is to focus in-depth on a specific case or a few cases, say, athletics – as it receives one of the highest funding packages – and, say, cycling, one of the most successful in terms of Olympic medals);
- reassure ourselves that there is not already a wealth of literature positing exactly the same question as we are.

Box 10   The literature review: an ongoing, reflexive process

Remember that the literature review has different purposes at different times during your project. We have identified three key stages:

1 The 'dip' into the literature in order to get a feel for what has and crucially what has *not* been written about your topic area.

2 The RQ or hypothesis-building stage: you should now be in a position to narrow your focus of literature significantly from stage 1, above. The purpose here is to finish with general RQs or tentative hypotheses.

3 The critical literature review, undertaken with your RQ(s) and/or hypothesis in mind. Refrain from simply listing the books, articles and proponents who have dealt with your topic area. Give a *clear* indication of their strength, their weaknesses and how they fit with your ideas and approach.

RQ = Research Question

In your literature reviews you should avoid developing a 'thinly disguised annotated bibliography' (Hart, 2000: 1) in the place of a proper, and critical, review of the literature. The purpose is to engage with the current literature, and to use it to develop your own approach and argument by critically analysing and flagging up the ideas you find fruitful, or not fruitful. You should not be presenting the reader with a giant book review, simply regurgitating in the form of a synopsis the contents of each book you have laid your hands on (Fred said this, Jane said that, etc.).

After undertaking a literature review with the revised research question in mind, to discipline your reading further, you can now return to the drawing board and redefine it. We would now write our essay, already knowing where we stand on our research question ('Can success in elite sport bring the UK "international prestige" and generate a "feel-good" factor among its citizens?'), how others, including the UK government, argue and present this rationale for elite sport investment, and how we are going to put forward an argument that the government's aim of obtaining 'international prestige' and generating a 'feel-good factor' among UK citizens as a result of elite sport success rests, as it does, more on hope than on any actual evidence.

● How to use the literature gathered, when writing an essay

Many students attract low marks by the manner in which they use literature in their essays. The first thing to avoid is producing an annotated book review in which you deal with authors and what they have to say on a particular topic one after the other (unless, of course, this is the express purpose of your task). There is nothing worse than having a student list 10 books in their bibliography, but then go on to either (a) cite great chunks from single sources in the essay, leaving the marker wondering whether they have actually read any of the other works listed, or (b) offer a blow-by-blow account of what each author said on the topic, throughout the essay (i.e. not 'integrating' the thoughts around specific themes). So, on our 'drugs in sport' example, we would first get three paragraphs on what Fred has to say on it – he's very much against the use of drugs in sport – then two from Jane – who opposes drugs, but cannot see the point of attempting to police it – and so on, with no connecting train of thought combining the works. Actually, there is something worse than the examples above: third-year undergraduates handing in essays with just three or four recognisable sources, which is unacceptable at degree level.

This is where our 'categorising' comes in handy; it may be slightly artificial in the sense of where one can precisely draw the line between a 'top-down' and 'bottom-up' approach or between someone focusing on 'structures' (say, organisations) and another on 'actors' (say, important or influential individuals in those organisations). For the purpose of setting up an argument and setting out how your essay fits in with what already exists, 'broad-brush' categorising can be very useful in structuring your review, so long as it is based on some identifiable 'pattern'. The example above of simply listing authors sequentially will generally not allow for the development of an argument, as the literature is not 'integrated' into the essay. This is not just a college or first-year undergraduate mistake: advanced undergraduates and even postgraduates make a similar mistake. One of the worst PhDs read by one of the authors did just this: the work contained a huge book review of relevant literature without any categorising or any notion of whether the student agreed, disagreed or was indifferent to the work being discussed. This point is valid for all students: whatever it is you are writing, you will generally need an opinion. Such an opinion ought to be based on knowledge (i.e. a reading and understanding of the literature around a topic) and should be distinguished from the pub-level 'opinion'. Students starting out generally have a problem with articulating their 'opinion'. One of the hardest things for new students beyond 'A' level is learning that 'knowledge' is not cut and dried

Avoid pub-level opinion

– i.e. views on, well, everything in the social world can be contested and there is no clear-cut 'right' or 'wrong'. However, in an essay the student needs to come down on one side or the other or propose a different view. The point is you need to make a point.

● Tips on reading and recording notes

It may seem daft having a short section on 'how to read', given that most of you reading this chapter have already mastered this skill. The ability to read is one thing; *how* to read is quite another. Many research study-skills books warn students not to read too much. There is something of a paradox here, although our advice would be not to get into the habit of burning the midnight oil, as a healthy life-style, including a good night's sleep, is the key to success. If you are out late every night of the week, you'll be too tired to concentrate and concentration is, unfortunately, what is needed when reading. What is meant when authors advise you not to read too much is that you need to become skilled in *how* you read; it is not so much the volume, it is *what* you read and *how* you read it that matters. We subscribe to the traditional wisdom – based as it is on empirical evidence in the form of years of personal experience – that there is a correlation between students who read the most widely and those who get the best marks, best exam results and degree classification, etc. That said, there is a skill to reading for an essay or project, which is usually carried out under tight time constraints. The first skill, which really can only be developed once you know what it is you are looking for ('literature review II'), could be termed 'skimming' the literature. It sounds lazy, but it is a time-efficient method of ascertaining whether a specific piece of literature is of any use to you and your essay. The first rule of skimming is: don't read the whole book, chapter or article; instead go straight to:

- the abstract (for an article, this is the summary at the beginning, usually 150–200 words long; for a report, look for the 'executive summary');
- the contents page (for a book, edited book, report etc.);
- the conclusion (article, book, book chapter, report summary);
- the index (book, edited book; look for key words – 'drugs', 'drugs and sport', 'drugs ban' etc. in our example).

You should be able to tell within three minutes whether this piece of literature is of any use to your project, instead of wasting hours wading through unnecessary, but fascinating, material.

Box 11   What is an essay and what is it for?

As all this literature gathering, note-taking and careful reading leads to the same thing – writing an essay of sorts – we thought it a good idea to tell you both what an essay is and what it is for.

The first thing to ask yourself is 'What is an essay?' and 'What is it for?' Ideally, an essay at college or university level in the UK is a piece of work containing a reasoned argument about a specifically defined topic, delivered in legible English, drawing upon a range of recognisable sources and following the conventions of attributing these sources, as set out by your institution. What it is not – this helps understand what it is – is an opinion-piece based on gut-feelings and information gathered in the student bar the night before the hand-in date.

Why do universities force poor students to answer such tricky questions as 'What is culture?' in the traditional form of the essay? It is not just for the fun of putting them through a nerve-wracking exercise, actually requiring students to make an effort. First off, it is a very good way of assessing a person's grasp of a subject and of the arguments and debates around a specific topic – hence the role of the literature review. Second, it reinforces the learning process – funnily enough, being made to research, think about, construct and present an argument, means we internalise much more of the subject matter than is the case when just reading. Good essay questions will test factual knowledge of a subject, but will also touch on conceptual issues or problems with which you'll be asked to grapple. A good research question ought to do the same.

Other skills essay writing teaches are:

- retrieving and researching the points relevant to the argument/ puzzle in the essay from an array of information sources;
- the ability to condense a large amount of information into a coherent and structured format – usually prescribed and limited by word-count (this is where 'categorising' comes in handy);
- to think critically about what you put in the essay, how you adjudicate between competing claims (or approaches) to the same phenomena;
- the skills to find your own voice (note this is not the same as 'I reckon, right ...'), based on a variety of sources and reasoned against other, competing arguments (hence the need to read 'around' a topic).

● Taking note of note-taking

When undertaking your literature review it is a *very* good idea to take clear notes from the start, indicating which book the notes are from, the author, place of publication etc. (see Chapter 6 for full referencing details). Take great care at this stage to distinguish between *your* notes of others' work and direct copying of quotes or sections. There is nothing wrong with the latter, if you clearly flag up that this is indeed the case, with relevant page numbers and other details. There are two dangers to the lazy or careless student and scholar: one is that three months down the line they can no longer tell where their own notes or words end and the words and phrases of the book's author begin. The other is that an idea read months before with no notes taken suddenly becomes germane to the student's or scholar's own thinking (this can happen when you study over a longer period of time), as different and diverse sets of ideas and facts begin to 'connect'. Both cases could lead to the accusation of plagiarism, the crime of all crimes in the world of ideas and academia (see Chapter 6 for more on this). So, if you read something that sets you off thinking, always note down where you have the original inspiration from. Let's say, in our early reading for the essay on 'drugs in sport', we come across a controversial stance which suggests that performance-enhancing drugs are no worse than the 'natural advantages' that some athletes have like living at altitude or having a certain genetic make-up. If we do not take proper notes at the time of reading, we may use this argument in our essay on the topic months later without reference to its origin, because we think that this is now in fact our own idea. Immediate and clear note-taking during reading, whether it is a year, month or week before the essay is due to be submitted, will prevent any accusation of plagiarism (see Cashmore, 2003, for an example of a controversial view on drugs in sport).

Summary

This chapter discussed:

☐ The role of the literature review in research.

☐ The need to categorise the literature you collect to help you structure your review.

☐ The need to 'place' your essay or view within the existing literature and debates around your chosen topic.

☐ Finally, we touched briefly on the art of reading; it's no good amassing all the literature around a topic and then becoming swamped. Remember: take careful notes of the literature as you read it and be very careful how you record the details, ideas, phrases and quotes, especially at this early stage.

Part II

Finding Resources:
What, Where and How

3 Online Resources Provided by Libraries and the Academic Community, part 1: Journals and Books

This chapter looks at:

▶ How to evaluate both print and online resources

▶ How to use online library catalogues to find the materials you need

▶ How to locate online journals and books

▶ How to use bibliographic databases to find out what has been published on a particular topic

⬤ Introduction

'You don't need to bother with the Library, it's all on the Internet now' is a statement you will often hear at university or college. It is true that the advent of the Internet and online sources has fundamentally changed the way in which research is undertaken, but there is still a vast number of resources that are only available in print or microfilm or with limitations to online access (of which more later). An important response to the statement above would be 'What do you mean by the Internet?' Over the last few years masses of traditional library materials have become available online; you can now do a literature review for journal articles from your computer without the danger of heavy index volumes falling on you from the shelves and the tedium of tracking down printed journals in dusty library **stacks**. It is not just a matter of convenience; all these traditional resources have, in effect, a quality mark stamped on them by years of usage in the academic and library world. Before many of them even reached a library they had been assessed by editors, and then they were subjected to further selection by librarians and academics. They have a tried and tested value and it is clear who has produced them and why. In the 'Information Landscape' diagram presented below (Figure 3.1), the traditional resources are shown as a select section of 'The Web' – in the rest of which, anyone can put anything without any quality assurance whatsoever. Such research and information gathering complements and often overlaps with the more

The Information Landscape

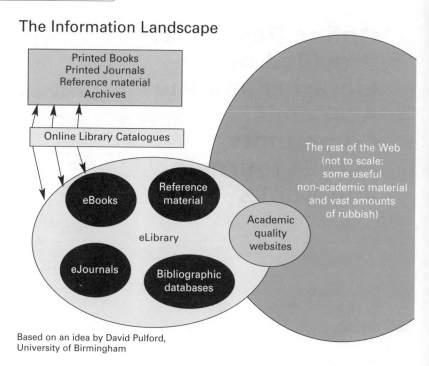

Based on an idea by David Pulford,
University of Birmingham

Figure 3.1   The Information Landscape

'traditional' literature search and review discussed in the previous chapter. The tips on reading and categorising material, given for traditional sources, are relevant for online sources as well. This chapter will look at how you can find and evaluate online resources within the traditional library world and also use various means to sift out the quality websites from the less useful material on the Web. Always bear in mind the words of the Internet Detective: 'The quality of information on the Internet is extremely variable. At best the Internet is a great research tool, at worst it can seriously degrade your work by feeding you misinformation' (Internet Detective, 2009). (The Internet Detective is a website giving advice on how to search and evaluate the Web; more details are available in Chapter 4.) Even if you only use the good material you will still have to keep your critical faculties active. A government departmental website may have good **provenance** and accurate content, but if it is aimed at the general public, it may not be the best source for a researcher.

Libraries use all sorts of different names for online sources; look for one of those in the list below. Better still, be really proactive and adventurous and ask a librarian. Various terms used include:

- Electronic resources
- e-Resources
- eResources
- eLibrary
- Online Resources
- Online Library
- Digital Library

(Please note that 'e' is for Electronic and has nothing to do with drugs or food additives whatsoever.)

How to evaluate both print and online resources

The format (print or online) of the resources you use is much less important than their academic quality and the analytical skills you bring to bear on finding and using them. The traditional resources in both formats start off with a big advantage in that there has usually been some thought given to their selection in the first place and they were selected by academic staff or librarians who knew the subject area. There are exceptions, of course, like out-of-date material (a work on hazardous chemicals from 1972, for example, is hazardous because of what it does not include). Also, libraries sometimes buy everything there is in a topic as a research collection – due to budget and space considerations this is a rare occurrence. However, a good example would be specialist collections of pre-1991 Soviet material from the USSR, where huge amounts of state-subsidised publications in many languages could be bought cheaply. As a presentation of a now past world viewpoint they can be fascinating, but you would not want to uncritically accept everything in such works.

Once you wander out into the wider Web you do not have even this basic level of quality assurance. You have to evaluate the sources (which often do not have basic details like author or date) as well as decide how relevant they are to your work. The unmediated Web seems 'easier' than the print and online library, especially if the goal is to assemble as many unsubstantiated sources as possible and cobble something together. Unfortunately, the opposite is required at college and university level (and in the future world of work), with the idea being to produce work based on reliable sources that has had some thought and analysis put into it. In addition, the sources used have to be traceable by anyone reading the work, so that they can form their own opinions of it (see Chapter 6 on referencing and plagiarism). In effect, the traditional sources are doing some of the analysis already.

Fortunately there are six simple questions you can ask about every resource you come across, whatever form it comes in. They are summarised in this extract from a poem by Rudyard Kipling (Kipling, 1940: 605):

> I keep six honest serving-men
> (They taught me all I knew);
> Their names are What and Why and When
> And How and Where and Who.

(*Note*: bringing in something unlikely, but in this case highly relevant, like Kipling, is the sort of odd twist that the authors use to keep you reading. And, by the way, he is nothing to do with the Mr Kipling cakes on supermarket shelves.)

You do not have to ask every question about everything you look at, but once you start getting unsatisfactory answers to basic questions like: *Who* wrote this? *Why* did they write it? *When* did they write it? then it will be time to look at something else. You do not want to rely on something when you

Kipling's six honest serving-men

have little or no idea of the author's expertise or credentials, their motivation, or if they have kept their work up-to-date. Apply the questions often enough and it will become second nature to evaluate everything without even thinking about it.

To show that there is no anti-Web bias at work here, let us apply some of these questions to the following print resource held in a very traditional library:

Author	Antisionnistskii komitet sovetskoi obshchestvennosti.
Added Entry	Criminal alliance of zionism and nazism.
Title	Criminal alliance of zionism and nazism: press conference of the Anti-Zionist Committee of Soviet Public Opinion, October 12, 1984.
Publisher	Moscow: Anti-Zionist Committee of Soviet Public Opinion, 1985.

Just asking *who* produced this, *why* they did and *when* and *where* is enough for you to start to treat this pamphlet about a Jewish/Nazi conspiracy against the Soviet Union during the Second World War with a little caution. There are far weirder things out there on the Web, with fewer clues as to their origins.

● Finding and using online resources via the services provided by libraries and the academic community

The way in which libraries make resources available to you may vary slightly in different universities and colleges, but they all contain the major elements described in this section. All libraries are constrained by conditions imposed by the publishers of these online sources, which restrict access to members of the institutions that have subscribed to them, and this can seem confusing to anyone used to the free-for-all approach on the Web. There is a parallel with printed books and journals; you have to be a registered member of the library to borrow them and there are security measures to ensure that they are not removed from the library building without being properly issued.

Basically, there are two methods of ensuring someone is entitled to use an online resource: passwords and **IP addresses**.

● Passwords

These can be a special password for a particular database, but most work on a system that uses the institutional username and

Online resources have 'protection'

password instead – cutting down the number of passwords you have to remember. Occasionally (all right, slightly more than occasionally), glitches in the system will reveal the mechanism behind this, and messages about mysterious things like **Athens** or **Shibboleth** will appear on the screen – do not worry about this; simply contact your library or computing helpdesk.

● **IP addresses**

Every computer has an Internet Protocol address; a sort of postcode for computers. Many online suppliers do not use password access and instead limit usage of their products to the IP addresses of the subscribing institution, which prevents anyone accessing them from home or other off-campus locations. The way round this is often to use something called a **proxy server**, which routes everything to the off-campus location via a server on campus which has the correct IP address. Only people with authentic institutional usernames and passwords can sign up for this service so it is not cheating (honestly). In order for the proxy service to work, you have to adjust your browser settings according to the instructions given by your institution's IT staff. Using the proxy often slows down the Internet connection, so it is a good idea to only use the proxy when you are accessing online materials provided by your university or college, and switch it off for the rest of the time.

One major problem will be encountered by 'continuing professional development' and other distance learners who want to access material via computers at their workplace. Places such as schools and social work departments often have **firewalls** that prevent the setting up of a proxy service and any attempt to do so may result in a visit from an angry systems manager. Most institutions usually have details in their library and resources web pages about **off-campus access** (a much more obvious term than 'proxy server'), so check the details in these pages, or ask at the library.

You may be lucky enough to be going to a university or college that has installed software that means you do not have to adjust your browser settings and just need to log in with a username and password. The proxy server is still there, however, even if you are not aware of it, and any problems with it will prevent access.

If you are using a laptop on campus you will need to have it configured to the local system, so that it has a valid local IP address. This is to prevent anyone just wandering onto a university campus and using the resources via their laptop; both the university authorities and publishers would not approve of this. Contact your library or computing helpdesk to find out how this can be done.

● Library catalogues

This is the most traditional way of finding resources in a library. A major change in recent years is that catalogues are now online and you can search them from outside the library and also do things like reserving and renewing books without having to physically visit the library. You can also look in the catalogues of other libraries to find difficult-to-obtain items, or libraries that are nearer to your home. You could also do this to assess, in advance, the colleges and universities you apply to. The University of Exeter has an online *Directory of UK Higher Education and Research Libraries* to help you find library websites:

www.library.ex.ac.uk/internet/uklibs.html

In addition, the Higher Education and Research Opportunities (HERO) directory has a list of libraries at:

www.hero.ac.uk/uk/reference_and_subject_resources/institution_facilities/
online_library_catalogues3792.cfm

HERO also has a list of Further Education Colleges:

www.hero.ac.uk/uk/reference_and_subject_resources/further_education/
fe_colleges3786.cfm

although many of these do not make their catalogues and online resources available for outsiders to look at, as a student log-on is often needed.

Catalogues usually try to include everything the library has, including printed and online books, printed and online journals, CDs, DVDs, maps, and so on. Some materials such as archives are difficult to list in the main catalogue and you may need to use a different one. Some older books, especially in libraries that have been around a long time, may not be listed in the online catalogue and you will have to go back to card indexes to find these. It is possible to scan these old index cards and some libraries may have the oddity of a card catalogue online as a temporary measure until they can be included in the main catalogue.

When searching for a book, always put in as many details as possible. If you just type in a title, especially a general one like *History of India*, you might get a long list; if you add the author Romila Thapar, you just get that particular book. This is a general point about online searching that applies well beyond simple library catalogues: *the best result comes from using specific terms and putting in as many as possible.*

Check to see if the reading lists for your course are in the catalogue; this means you don't have to search for each item individually – just go into the list and select the item you want and it will link to the relevant details in the catalogue.

Once you start to get beyond prescribed reading you will need to start using catalogue search options like **keyword** and **classification** to find what the library has on a particular subject. The library catalogue, even in its online form, has a major disadvantage when doing detailed subject searches. It indexes the *titles* of books and journals, but not their *content* – in other words it can tell you the library has *The Economist* from 1950 onwards and where it is in the library, but it tells you nothing about the articles within it. *What* is the catalogue searching? Usually just the words in titles, book authors/editors and some **subject headings** added when the book was catalogued. There is an answer to this: use **bibliographic databases** (see below).

● Online journals and books

Journal articles are at the very heart of the academic process as they concentrate on very specific subject areas and are the place where academic debates take place and ideas and theories develop. Having journal articles readily accessible online has rapidly become a major part of the academic world and most librarians will tell you that practically every library usage/satisfaction survey includes requests for 'more online journals'.

In addition, many libraries are now so full that they do not put new issues of journals on the shelves, if there is an online equivalent. If you don't find out how to access the online journals, you are cut off from a major research resource, including the cutting edge of your particular area of interest.

The move to making books available online is more recent, but it is gathering apace. Factors still holding it back include difficulties if reading large amounts of text online, and restrictions on downloading the full text from online books. It is very important that you find out how your library organises access to online journals and books. In some there are links to these from within the library catalogue; in others they are in a separate eLibrary (or equivalent term).

Using online journals

There are two main ways of finding the online journals and articles you need, according to whether you know the journal you want, or want to find what has been published on a particular subject. First, we will look at how to find a journal article you have been told about; further on in this chapter we will look at finding journal articles (plus other resources like book chapters and conference papers) on a subject of your choice.

If you have been told there is a particular article you need, or want to browse through the latest articles in a journal that is important in your area of interest, you just look up the *title of the journal* (not the title of the article) in the library catalogue or the eLibrary (or its equivalent in your institution).

As an example, you might need to read this article: Biehal, N. (2008) 'Preventive Services for Adolescents: Exploring the Process of Change', *British Journal of Social Work*, 38 (3): 444–61.

Biehal is the name of the author, the article is 'Preventive Services for Adolescents: Exploring the Process of Change' and it was published in the *British Journal of Social Work* in 2008. The numbers 38 (3): 444–61 refer to the volume number of the journal, the part number and the pages of the article within that part, respectively. The terms 'volume' and 'part' are relics of the print past, but they are useful in locating the online version of an article, as we shall see. The part is the individual issue of a journal which are usually published up to 6 times a year, although the gaps between them can be longer or shorter. The volume is traditionally the bound version of all these parts, usually one per year, but with chunkier journals there might be more than one volume in a year.

First you type *British Journal of Social Work* (the title of the journal) into the relevant search box in the Library Catalogue or the eLibrary (depending on the access arrangements at your college or university). You may find there are several different sources available for this title. When choosing the one you want it is important to note the dates covered, for example in this case you might have two alternatives:

Chadwyck PAO: 1971–1995
Oxford University Press Journals: 1971–

As you want a date in 2008 you need to choose the open-ended option and select Oxford University Press Journals. This will take you to the *British Journal of Social Work* page in the publisher's website, where you then have to track down the issue you want. Publishers have several ways of listing the issues on their sites, the most common are these:

- The latest issue is featured on the home page and if you want to find anything older you have to locate an 'archive' or similar term – even if the issue you want is only a few months, or years old. Oxford University Press is one of these, so just click on 'Browse archive'.
- All the issues are listed in one nice, simple list and you just scroll down the list to find the one you want.
- The really awkward publishers take you to a general home page, rather than a page for each journal title, and you have to search for the journal you want and then locate the issues.

Having got into the *British Journal of Social Work* archive you select the relevant issue (38, part 3). Doing this takes you to an online contents list, which you scroll down to find the article by Biehal. Articles are still listed in page number order, even though they are online.

In this case, but not always with other publishers, you have a choice of two versions of the article to read: Full Text or **PDF**. This is a bit puzzling, because both versions give you the full text of the article. Oxford University Press use 'Full Text' to mean the **HTML** version, whilst most other publishers use it to mean anything in full text. PDF is visually the same as a printed page and this is often easier to read. HTML has links to references and enables the reader to navigate around a long article by going straight to each section within it, but line lengths and typeface may make it tiring to read for long periods of time.

Using online books

The number of online books/eBooks available is rapidly increasing, although they are still not as dominant as online journals. There are two main points you need to grasp when using them. The first is how access to them is arranged in your institution, either by direct links from titles of individual books in the library catalogue, or by large collections in the eLibrary, where you have to search each collection separately. Major commercial collections which need a subscription include *ebrary*, *MyiLibrary* and *Oxford Scholarship Online*. Free eBook collections include *Google Books* and *Project Gutenberg*.

The second important point is to be aware of how the eBook has been created. Some collections such as *EEBO* (*Early English Books Online*) are just digitised images of the books, so that you cannot search within the text of the books. Most collections do have the facility to search within the text, and in many cases you can make your own notes. You should also be aware that texts that have been scanned may contain inaccuracies, such as 'rn' being reproduced as 'm'. (On the website there is an account of the life of someone named Cockburn, who is referred to throughout as Cockbum.)

There may also be some technical points that you need to look out for. With *ebrary*, for example, you need to download some software in order to see the text. A major drawback with eBooks is that there are limits on how much you can print from books at a time. *Ebrary*, for example, limits each printing session to a maximum of five pages of the original book, which works out at less on standard A4 printing paper. The publishers are very good at keeping track of who is downloading what.

In the free ebook collections such as *Google Books* you cannot view the full text of books still in **copyright**. Everything in *Project Gutenberg* is available in full text because it has only material that is out of copyright, although even here there is a snag as they are out of US copyright, but may still be copyright in the UK. With eBook collections available via your library, the subscriptions paid give access to the full text.

EBook providers also have an irritating obsession with providing 'packages' of books; not with providing individual titles that are in high demand, because they are on reading lists or classics in their field. Often large numbers of titles disappear from the package and are replaced by others; very annoying when you need to consult a book a few months later and it has gone and there is no print version available in your library. There is a parallel here with the instability of content on government websites when looking for official publications.

● Finding what has been published on a topic in books and journals: bibliographic databases

Finding online journal articles and books when you know details such as the title and author already is relatively straightforward, once you have got a grip on how your institution's library arranges access and you are not deterred by the varying terminology and page layout used by different publishers. When you want to find what has been published on a particular subject you will need to use **bibliographic databases**, which index academic quality publications.

Bibliographic databases get behind the titles of books and journals and reveal the contents. By using them you can find individual articles in journals, papers in conference proceedings, and individual book chapters. These databases produce **abstracts** that summarise what each work is about, and index the articles by using standardised terms. This abstracting and indexing is done by actual real thinking people, rather than the automated processes of a search engine, which look at the words out of context.

Even so, you still have to think carefully about what you want when searching; words are slippery things and on at least one occasion a politics student has looked for 'arms control' and found articles on artificial limbs. Try these methods to clarify your thought and search processes:

- Find out what words and concepts *mean* in the academic world; is it the same as what *you* think they mean? For this you can use encyclopaedias and dictionaries, and if possible these should be specialised works for your topic rather than general ones like *Encyclopaedia Britannica*. Online examples would be the *New Palgrave Dictionary of Economics* or the *International Encyclopaedia*

of the Social and Behavioural Sciences – but why not visit an actual
bookshelf if there's nothing available online.

- Think of alternative words to search for to increase the number of
  results you obtain. Think of synonyms, for example: 'teenagers',
  'adolescents' and 'young people'.

- Find out when terms and expressions came into or out of use. Find
  older terms or newer ones: whatever happened to 'joined-up
  government', which was all the rage around the turn of the
  Millennium? According to one author it came in with New Labour
  and was dropped in the party's second term (Caulkin, S. 2006: [1]).
  The cited reference is only a brief article in the *Observer*, but it
  already gives a likely time frame and some specific examples of
  joined-up government, or the lack of it. Also, beware of changes in
  both the names and responsibilities of organisations; especially
  government departments and agencies.

Online searching makes it all the more important to be very specific, as a
search can easily turn up thousands of results (some databases call these
hits). Bizarrely enough, the more search terms you put in, the fewer results
you get, as long as you ask the database to search for all the words. See the
example (Box 12 from a search done in a bibliographic database called *ASSIA
(Applied Social Sciences Index and Abstracts)*.

Box 12   Searching: where more equals less

Example is from *ASSIA (Applied Social Sciences Indexes and Abstracts)*
(search done on 8 July 2008)

- search for 'alcohol': 13692 articles which mention alcohol

- search for 'adolescents': 15161 articles which mention adolescents

- search for 'alcohol' *and* 'adolescents': 1344 articles which mention
  both alcohol *and* adolescents

- search for 'alcohol' *and* 'adolescents' *and* 'England': 15 articles
  which mention alcohol *and* adolescents *and* England

- go to the date range option and select 2002–2008: 12 articles which
  mention alcohol *and* adolescents *and* England *and* were published
  between 2002 and 2008

Always try to use the Advanced Search option in a bibliographic database; 'Quick' or 'Simple' searches are no such things in the long run if you can't cope with wading though the mass of irrelevant material you get.

Features common to most online bibliographic databases

- **Ways to make your searching more accurate**   Look for something like 'search tips' to see how your database copes with alternative spellings ('organise' and 'organize'). Also how you can enter a phrase; in the *Web of Science* bibliographic database, putting double quotation marks around the phrase "North Sea" means it looks for just that and ignores the words North and Sea when they occur on their own – if they were included you would get masses of stuff that have nothing to do with the North Sea and would include irrelevancies like North Carolina or the Dead Sea. This method may not apply to other databases, so you need to check what each one does.

- **Abstracts**   Those paying attention will remember these from Chapter 2 – they can be very handy when 'skimming' the literature. Abstracts are summaries of the article's contents and enable you to judge whether the article you have found is relevant to your study. The search terms that you have entered are often highlighted in the abstract, so that you can check whether the article is using them in the same way as you; i.e. that it is about 'arms control' in the international law sense and not about artificial limbs. Also, the abstract may provide extra information – for example, the article may be a perfectly good one about teenage pregnancies in Sweden, but you want to focus on the UK. In the past, abstracts saved a lot of wasted time and effort tracking down printed journal articles on library shelves, which turned out not to be relevant, and they can still save you wasted time and effort, not to mention keeping your printing costs down.

- **Links to full text**   Most bibliographic databases can now link you to the full text of the article, but this only works when your institution has a subscription to the online version. If not, you may be offered a link to the relevant entry in the library catalogue for a print version, or even to the catalogues of other libraries.

- **Save details such as title, issue, year etc., for references**
  In most bibliographic databases you can do this by just ticking a box – you never have to get the details wrong again. Read more about this and also ways to use referencing software, in Chapter 6 on 'Referencing and Plagiarism'.

- **Updating services**   These enable you to get details of new arti-cles and other materials as they come out. This might well save you from the embarrassment of putting a lot of effort into a piece of work and then having your supervisor ask, 'What effect do you think the recently proposed government policy is likely to have on this?', and all you can say is 'What government policy?'
  You need to register with each database (free if you are using it via your university or college) for these services. The names for these services can vary widely, for example, *ASSIA* has plain and simple 'My Research', whilst *Web of Science* has 'Customize Your Experience'.
  There are two main ways in which you can be updated:

  - **Saving and rerunning searches**: You can re-do the same search a few weeks later and find the new articles published.
  - **Alerts**: By this method the database will email you every time something new is added that fits your saved search strategy.

Examples of some important bibliographic databases

Look in your eLibrary for these; many libraries list what is available for each subject so browse around and find others. It is essential to use more than one source for anything (as we suggested in Chapter 2), so look in something general like *Web of Science* and also something more specific to your subject. Note: there are no **URLs** (Internet addresses) given here; if you go direct into any of these using the Internet address they will not recognise your right to use them and will ask you for passwords and usernames and try to charge you for downloading articles. *Always* access this type of database via your institution, if it has a subscription to it.

- *JSTOR* is a large collection of journals in a wide range of disciplines, wih an emphasis on arts and humanities and the social sciences. It is an archive of older issues, so you will not find material from recent years; on the other hand some of the periodical runs date back to the nineteenth century. It is not a bibliographic database as such, but does include useful features like full text searching.

- *LION* (*Literature online*) has the full text of several thousand works of American and English poetry, drama and prose, as well as literary journals and critical works. It also contains the *MLA* (*Modern Language Association*) *Bibliography*, covering language and linguistics.

- *Web of Science* is probably the most misleadingly named database ever, as it covers all subjects including social sciences, arts and humanities, as well as science and technology. It may appear in your eLibrary as *Social Sciences Citation Index* or *Arts and Humanities Index* or even as *Web of Knowledge*. It is huge and covers only peer-reviewed journals. These are journals which have an academic board who send submitted articles to other academics to review, thereby maintaining academic standards (in theory). Although it is restricted to journal articles, you can find books in your subject because these journals include book reviews. A major feature of *Web of Science* is the citations; every article covered has a list of other articles cited in it and also of articles citing the one you are looking at. Thus, if you come across an article published in 2005, and providing that it is any good, you should be able to get the background and broader context by looking at the older articles cited in it, and follow the academic debate into more recent years. The citing author may expand on the article or they may completely refute it and say it is rubbish (but in a polite and thoroughly scholarly way, of course).

Web of Science attempts to cover every academic subject, but inevitably there are gaps and it is important to look at more specialised databases concerned solely with your subject. Many of them cover non-peer-reviewed journals, unlike *Web of Science*, and you can often trace conference papers, book chapters and other works in them. The examples given below are the major ones, but explore your online library or speak to a librarian to find others.

- *ASSIA* (*Applied Social Sciences Index and Abstracts*) is a major source for publications in the area of social work and social policy. It includes works in several related fields, such as criminology, psychology, and health services management, from a social work and social policy point of view, for example, memory and ageing. It comes from the same publisher as *Sociological Abstracts* and you can search both at the same time if necessary. Even more specialised databases for social work and policy include *AgeInfo*, specialising in works about all aspects of ageing, and *Childlink*, doing something similar about children.

- *Sociological Abstracts* is the major source for sociology and because it comes from the same publisher as *ASSIA* it has the same search screen layout and you can search both databases at the same time.

- *British Education Index* deals with research, policy and practice in education and training in the UK. For a similar coverage of education from an American point of view, try *ERIC* (*Educational Resources Information Centre*).

- *Business Source Premier* and *ProQuest* are major databases for business and management, although they can be of use for economics students as well. Due to the nature of the subject, they index things like directories, case studies and market research as well as the usual journals and books.

- *EconLit* covers economics literature, hence the name. In addition to the usual journal articles it indexes dissertations and working papers. *EconLit*'s service for re-doing searches and getting alerts is called My EBSCOhost.

- *Historical Abstracts* covers the history of the world (excluding the United States and Canada) from 1450 to the present, including topics such as world history, military history, women's history and the history of education. Fill the American history gap with *Humanities Abstracts* and the *MLA International Bibliography*.

- In bibliographic databases for law, the content devoted to legislation, law reports and other sources is as important as the indexing of journal articles. Major examples include *Lawtel*, for UK law, and *Westlaw*, which covers European Union and other foreign legislation in addition to the UK.

- *IBSS* (*International Bibliography of the Social Sciences*) is especially useful for politics and international studies, as it indexes a higher proportion of foreign-language works than most other databases available in UK eLibraries.

Summary

☐ Always evaluate every resource you use, regardless of whether it is print or online or if it comes from the library or the World Wide Web.

☐ The online resources provided by libraries and the academic community have been developed over many years and they can provide the right tools for the job of creating valid academic work.

☐ Make sure you know how to gain access to the online journals and books at your university or college.

☐ Most, but not all, academic journals are now available online, whilst eBooks are still much less common, although the numbers are increasing.

And finally ... with any resource, be it printed or online, always remember to:

Evaluate! Evaluate! Evaluate!
(and then Evaluate again).

4 Online Resources Provided by Libraries and the Academic Community, part 2: Other Resources

This chapter looks at:

► How to locate subject gateways for finding websites of sufficient quality to be used in academic work
► 'Open Access' to academic journals and other publications
► How to locate statistics
► How to locate official publications
► The whereabouts of online archives

● Introduction

Online journals and books are two of the main resources for academic work, but there is also a wide variety of other resources that you can access online. The web pages of government departments, academic research projects, non-governmental organisations, professional associations and other organisations often have material that is of a standard that can be used in your work. These can be traced using online subject gateways, which are better adapted to locating academic-level information than search engines.

In recent years the **Open Access** movement has made many academic journals, research papers, working papers and theses available free on the Internet, with no need to authenticate with passwords and so forth.

However, there are still limitations to what is available for free on the Internet and this chapter looks at the reasons for this and discusses examples from important resources such as official publications, statistics and archives.

● Subject gateways: use them to get at the good stuff on the Internet

Subject gateways are a means of finding material on the Internet that is of a sufficiently high standard to be included in academic work. You will find many of them in eLibraries/online libraries.

Subject gateways originated in the early days of the Internet with individual researchers bookmarking their favourite websites and useful sources of online information. A bigger than usual example of one of these is *Richard Kimber's Political Science Resources* www.psr.keele.ac.uk/ (a useful place to locate party election manifestos when they disappear from the parties' websites after the election).

Experts selecting and evaluating good quality reliable resources has remained a distinguishing feature of subject gateways to this day. When compared with search engines like Google, subject gateways have the following features:

- Resources are selected on the basis of their subject relevance.
- Standard indexing is used, so if you find one site that is relevant, you can find others.
- The selection and indexing is done by information professionals and academics who know their own subjects.
- The reputation and academic standing of the sites is taken into account; each is organised and evaluated for good **provenance**.

As a result you may get fewer results than with a search engine, but they are likely to be of much better quality and more relevance.

Box 13   From an information skills training session at the University of Birmingham

Librarian: Subject gateways take into account the reputation and academic standing of websites and the sites are evaluated for good provenance. In other words, anything produced by nutters in their bedrooms is excluded.

Student: There are a lot of nutters here at the University.

Librarian: Yes. But they're a better class of nutter.

The major subject gateway for the British academic community is *Intute*. There are no restrictions to the use of this; it is available to everyone, whether they are in higher or further education, or members of the public. All you need to do is go direct to their website: www.intute.ac.uk/. Most of the resources listed are free, but each has a description that includes details of anything for which you need to pay. With the websites of professional organisations and academic societies there may be closed areas of the sites that only members can use. The description also indicates *who* is creating the site, its purpose (*why*), *when* it was created and often the methodology used (*how*).

You can search by the following:

- Subject area;
- Type of resource (for example, government bodies, professional organisations, blogs);
- Keyword;
- A combination of any of these.

Intute has an 'Editor's choice' (highlighted in yellow) which picks out the key websites in a subject. *Intute* is good for finding the sites of important government, academic and professional organisations, and these sites have articles, conference proceedings and other publications on them to supplement what you can get from bibliographic databases.

Intute's guidance on searching the Internet

In addition to cataloguing and indexing sites, *Intute* also has guidance on how to evaluate the Internet resources in your subject area. The Intute *Virtual Training Suite* offers self-paced tutorials for each academic subject:

www.vts.intute.ac.uk/

You can further sharpen your critical faculties and your ability to sort out 'The Good, the Bad and the Ugly' on the Internet by using the *Internet Detective* at:

www.vts.intute.ac.uk/detective/

If you discover a suitable website that isn't covered by *Intute*, and some or all of Kipling's Serving-Men agree, you can use the 'Suggest a site' option in *Intute* to bring it to their attention.

Other subject gateways

Try browsing in your eLibrary to find other subject gateways. Listed below are just a few examples (many of which have free access, so the Internet address is included).

- The *British Academy Portal* provides links to sites in a wide range of the humanities and social sciences, including history, economics, law, political studies, social anthropology and sociology.

  www.britac.ac.uk/portal/

- In addition to providing links to websites concerned with historical research, the *Institute of Historical Research* has a large number of free journal articles and contains a news section and details of new and forthcoming books.

  www.history.ac.uk/

- *REESWeb* is based at the University of Pittsburgh and provides annotated links to Russian and East European resources in all subject disciplines. If you find a useful site that is not already in *REESWeb* there is a 'Submission' section where you can ask for it to be added.

  www.ucis.pitt.edu/reesweb/

- The *Social Science Research Network* brings together several subject-based research networks in the social sciences. Registration is free and, whilst there are not many links, there are a lot of free papers and articles to download.

  www.ssrn.com

- The *Social Work Gateway* is hosted by the University of Southampton and, as its name implies, lists and describes websites on all aspects of social work. It has a useful section on 'Critical use of the WWW'.

  www.pantucek.com/swlinks_gb.html

● Finding free materials for your research: Open Access

The division between high quality material only available via subscription sources and low quality free material is starting to blur as a result of the Open Access movement. It has a strange parallel in the changes in the postal system in the nineteenth century, when the introduction of the postage stamp shifted the costs of posting from the recipient (the reader of the information) to the sender of the information. The new moves in academic publishing seek to shift the cost of access to quality research information to the authors of the materials (whether journal articles or book chapters, for example), making it free at the point of use to you, the reader (Suber, 2002 [unpaginated]). Even though the resources may be of academic quality, do not forget to carry on evaluating.

Locating free academic quality resources on the Internet

When trying to find quality research, but free resources, on the Internet, it helps to understand *how* this sort of material is published. Resources on open access either tend to be published in open access journals or they are stored in databases, often called 'repositories'. When these repositories are run by a university they are referred to as **institutional repositories** because they are a repository of the intellectual product of the institution. There are far fewer of these repositories in further education colleges as these tend to place less emphasis on research. However, material in institutional repositories is freely available to anyone, anywhere. In some cases there may be an embargo period before the full text is available, but there are few other restrictions.

The following are some of the main ways of locating this open access material; URLs (Internet addresses) are given as all these resources are freely available on the Internet:

- In the *Directory of Open Access Journals* you can browse for specific journals or search for articles using keywords. It can also be used to check if journals charge a fee to anyone submitting an article. This is the most comprehensive free journal listing:

  www.doaj.org

- There are many resources which can be used to search the various subject or institution-based repositories. Researchers may well have placed a copy of their peer-reviewed articles into one of these and they often have theses, working papers and other materials held by the sources listed below.

  - *OpenDOAR* lists, describes and indexes over 1100 digital subject-based repositories that are open to public searching. The coverage is worldwide. The odd spelling of DOAR is an acronym of Directory of Open Access Repositories.

    www.opendoar.org/

  - *Intute Repository Search* is part of *Intute* and can be used to search for research material in UK institutional repositories.

    www.intute.ac.uk/irs/

  - *DRIVER* cross-searches the content of European institutional and subject repositories to locate European research output including original data:

http://search3.driver.research-infrastructures.eu/
webInterface/simpleSearch.do?action=load

(This is yet another acronym: Digital Repository
Infrastructure Vision for European Research.)

- *OAIster* cross-searches the content of over 1000 repositories
worldwide:

www.oaister.org

- You could also try typing your subject area plus 'open access
journal' into a search engine and view the results. Search engines
have their uses.

● 'Oh no, it's not all on the Internet': what you cannot get online, or can only get with restrictions

It is frequently stated how amazing it is that there is so much online and so much more being added. The authors would not even think of contesting this, but with the important caveat that the level of quality and availability of online provision still has major gaps and restrictions on use. As will be shown in the examples that follow, these gaps and restrictions are not short term, but are caused by factors such as basic economics and the priorities of the information providers. Technological change may alter these, but researchers have to deal with the situation now – they cannot sit around waiting for things to improve.

● Statistics

Statistics are a good example of a resource which is available online, but not necessarily for free. Also, there may not be much in the way of historical depth – only recent figures may be online. Statistics are a key source for research in a wide range of disciplines and need to be used with more care and thought than that shown by an undergraduate who told one of the authors that he wanted 'some statistics to dress up my essay'. Collecting, analysing and making available good quality statistics takes a lot of time and effort; they do not 'just appear'. You need to think about *who* is collecting the data and *why* they are collecting it (and for *whom*?) in order to find the best resources and also to understand how online access to these resources is organised.

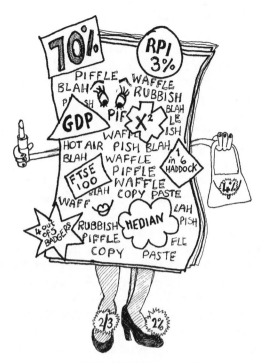

An essay 'dressed up' with statistics

● **Commercial sources of statistics**

Mintel and *MarketLine* are large databases that collect data on market research and produce reports on the market share of particular products and trends. That's *what* they are, and their *why* is to make money. There is no way they are going to let their valuable commercial information be free on the Web – someone has got to pay; and businesses are willing to pay (a lot) for information vital to them. There are (relatively) cheaper options for the further and higher education environment to make this data available, but researchers will have to use their 'eLibrary' (or equivalent), which ensures only members of the institution that pays for it get to use it.

These commercial suppliers of statistics are not just of use to the obvious fields of economics or business; anyone interested in public health could find all sorts of information in Mintel's data on trends in food consumption, for instance. When using the data, researchers have to remember that another basic fact about statistics, whether online or not, is *what* they are. In this case it is commercial information, which has to be adapted for other purposes.

● UK official statistics

The biggest producer of statistics in Britain is the government. The Census, taken every ten years since 1801 (except 1941), is the jewel in the crown, but every government department and agency produces masses of statistics as a result of its day-to-day work.

When it comes to making this data available online the situation is very confusing for the researcher. Each government department arranges its websites differently and the search mechanisms are not outstanding. Clearly labelled 'Statistics' sections are notable by their absence. The best bet is usually to go for the 'Publications' section, if there is one, as this often contains annual reports, research publications, government polices and the like.

It is also often difficult for the researcher to know which departments are producing the statistics she needs; where is the best place for child health statistics? The Department of Health, the NHS, the Department for Children, Schools and Families, all of them, or these and other departments? A valiant attempt at providing some cross-searchability of all statistical sources is provided by the UK Statistics Authority site (www.statistics.gov.uk/).

Hidden under the inscrutable heading 'UK snapshot' you can select data by broad subject themes such as Health and Care, or by entering search terms. The search produces a rather strange mixture of 'stories', 'articles', statistical sources and actual data in **CSV** or **Excel** formats and the researcher has to decide what they want from this. 'Stories' are usually less serious or data heavy than 'articles', apparently. One obvious point is that many of the sources do not go back very far in time, with the oldest online version of *Social Trends* being the 2002 edition. For anything earlier, with this and other statistical publications, it is a case of heading off to the shelves for a printed version, although the researcher might get lucky and find an online publication that contains a back run of figures.

At least the results of a search usually give some indication of the main suppliers of data in a particular area, even if links sometimes do not work due to the perennial problem of website redesign. Unfortunately the UK Statistics Authority site adds confusion by having additional sections on 'Neighbourhood' (local statistics), 'Economy', 'Census' and 'Population'.

One important point to remember about this site, and indeed most governmental sites, is that they have a one-size-fits-all approach to information provision: school children doing homework and senior academic researchers are all treated the same and have to pick out material at the level they need (*What* is being provided? *Who* is it provided for?).

The Neighbourhood Statistics site illustrates this approach well. It has a basic Neighbourhood Summary report of standard data for an area at a 'Wow, isn't that interesting' level. It also has a more detailed 'Finding Statistics' for an area, where the researcher can choose what she wants from a menu of datasets. This can be further elaborated with methods that enable the researcher to create her own areas for statistical data, creating graphs and charts, analysing data and so on. As with other sources of official statistics, and government websites in general, the time coverage is very shallow – just the 2001 census, plus some other data gathered since. The 'Census' section of the UK Statistics Authority site says with classic understatement, 'A limited selection of the findings of the 1991 Census are available online' (UK Statistics Authority, 2008). For most figures a simple comparison between 2001 and 1991 (and anything earlier) involves a trip to the printed versions.

For local statistical data (down to ward level and below) the situation is even worse, as it takes a lot of space to have all the printed *Small Area Statistics* for the whole country, and most libraries only have them for their own local area. Some libraries may still have the 1981 and 1991 censuses on CDRom, published by Chadwyck Healey, tucked away somewhere, which contain the small area statistics – it says a lot about government statistical provision that as recently as the mid-1990s they relied on outsourcing to commercial publishers for the electronic version of something as central to statistical provision as the Census.

● International statistics

At least the British government makes a lot of statistics available online for free. Researchers who want to access international data online come up against the problem that many international organisations, such as the OECD (Organisation for Economic Co-operation and Development), charge subscription fees for access.

One possibility is to go to the websites of foreign government statistical departments, and there are several online directories that can help with tracing these. The United Nations has a listing at:

http://unstats.un.org/unsd/methods/inter-natlinks/sd_natstat.asp

and the United States Census Bureau also has an international listing:

www.census.gov/main/www/stat_int.html

Other government departments also produce statistical data and a useful finding guide for these is *Intute*; particularly the Statistics and Data section:

www.intute.ac.uk/socialsciences/statistics/

Another source, which needs to be used with caution, as it has not been updated since 2002 (*When?*), is *Governments on the WWW* at:

www.gksoft.com/govt/en/

With sources such as this, *who* is collecting the data is usually fairly clear, but *why* can often lead to all sorts of questions about political bias and hidden governmental agendas. The *how*, when applied to many developing countries, raises questions of the resources available to pay for accurate data collection. There is also the important question: *why* is data collected by governments? In wealthier countries data is often collected as evidence to support the need for new facilities such as schools, hospitals etc. In some poorer countries there may be less need to collect accurate data to provide such evidence, as there is little money to pay for the new facilities (Carr-Hill, 2005, PowerPoint® slide 7).

In addition, the researcher needs to know the language of the original source, which can be a problem if several countries have to be compared. The US Census Bureau site does direct to any English-language version of the statistical websites, possibly because Americans are even worse at foreign languages than the British, but these are usually just brief introductory pages or sections, not the full data.

Data collected from national sources by international organisations such as the IMF (International Monetary Fund) and the United Nations overcomes this problem by bringing together all the national figures. There is often another benefit in that the figures are 'harmonised', with differences in the national sources' statistical methodologies being ironed out to make comparisons easier. The ILO (International Labour Organisation) produced unemployment figures for the UK throughout the 1980s and 1990s using one standard set of criteria, whilst the UK government controversially changed them several times (how *many* times being an interesting statistical enquiry in itself). Harmonisation is not a benefit, if the researcher wants to know *what* figures the individual government wants to make public; in this case national sources have to be used.

In Britain some of the major statistical series from the United Nations, IMF, World Bank, ILO and the OECD (Organisation for Economic Cooperation and Development) are available via *ESDS International*, a part of the *Economic and Social Data Service*. These are long runs, back into the early 1950s in some cases, which is good by online standards.

The limitation is that the data can only be used for free by the British academic community (anyone registered at a UK higher education institution); so just going to the web address and trying to get data is not going to work. Users have to access the service via the eLibrary and register to use it;

being logged in to their local system shows they are eligible to use *ESDS*. *How* is the data made available? By a national deal negotiated by **JISC** (Joint Information Systems Committee), who pay the data suppliers on behalf of UK higher and further education. *Why* is access limited? Because JISC is empowered to act for the higher education community, it is not a charity providing for all. In practice, most researchers do not know and do not care about all this – but it is all part of the online information environment within which they have to work.

The European Union has recently gone down the 'free access to statistics' route and these are available via the not very originally named *Eurostat* site (http://epp.eurostat.ec.europa.eu/), a very useful resource for the student of European affairs. There are two different levels of statistics:

- Tables: ready made general tables.
- Data: where you can construct tables step by step, selecting the information you want.

Like many online statistical resources there are problems getting older data, and the cut-off points can vary; plus there may not be any data from the period prior to a member country joining. The figures are harmonised for

International statistical comparison

comparative purposes and there are some figures from major non-EU countries, again for comparison.

The database is best searched by following the statistical 'themes'; for example, follow the Population and Social Conditions theme to the Health section. Within that there are two levels of information, ready-made tables, giving basic information, and the database, where you can select the factors you want to include.

Using the 'Health Status' heading you can retrieve statistics on obesity throughout the EU contained in the Health Information Survey 2004 (data collected 1999–2003), which includes measures of Body Mass Index. The percentages of those classified as obese range from 6.1% in Norway to the porkiest of the lot, 23% for Malta. The UK just manages to avoid the top spot at 22.7% and, despite all the cheese, paté and wine, the French only have 9.3% obese. These are just overall figures; it is possible to break them down further by age, occupational status, educational status and gender.

● Official publications

The policy documents and records of government departments and agencies are a major source for researchers across a wide range of subjects and disciplines. Yet the provision of these documents online by the UK government has been shambolic, to put it nicely.

The *Why?* question supplies a major reason. Most government websites are aimed at providing current information (*What?*) to the general public – not providing useful material for researchers (*Who?*). Take a look at the Department for Work and Pensions site (www.dwp.gov.uk/) or the Department for Children, Schools and Families (www.dcsf.gov.uk/) and you can see they are the online equivalent of the leaflet racks in government offices. Major policy documents are either not preserved or are very difficult to find (see the example 'The Case of the Missing Green Paper', Box 14, on p. 82). The Directgov site (www.direct.gov.uk/) is useful in providing an overview of government sites, but it also reinforces the absence of any special provision for academic research.

The National Archives site (www.nationalarchives.gov.uk/) is unusual in that it actually has a section specifically for academic researchers, although even with this site the homepage is dominated by facilities for family history and other popular topics.

Sometimes the lack of a 'joined-up' approach is quite astonishing. A researcher might well need to follow the progress of a piece of legislation and the reasons why it changed from the proposed Bill on its way to becoming an

Act of Parliament, or why it never made it into legislation at all. The various publications needed all have different online starting dates. The Bills (proposed legislation) are only available online for the current session; the Standing Committee debates are available from the 1997–98 session onwards; the House of Lords Hansard debates from 1995–96 onwards and the Commons equivalent from 1988–89 onwards. Tracing the passage of a piece of 1994 legislation would mean that you could read only the Commons Hansard debates online and you would need to have a print copy of the Bill next to the computer screen to make any sense of the amendments to the wording of individual clauses mentioned in the debates. For everything else you would have to head for the shelves. (Note: some cynical persons might say there is not much sense in the debates anyway.)

In 2007 some major steps forward were taken with a couple of JISC (Joint Information Systems Committee) sponsored deals; The *House of Commons Parliamentary Papers*, which covers 1685 to the current day, and *Public Information Online*, which starts in 2007. These at least preserve all major policy documents and Bills, amongst a wealth of other information. However, there are still anomalies; the latter is the only one to have House of Lords publications and neither has Hansard debates. A major point to remember is that these deals are only available to the academic community, so you have to use them via the eLibrary in your university or college – you cannot just get them off the Internet.

Plus, other documents published by individual government departments that do not form part of the parliamentary papers rely for their online existence upon the whims and practices of each department; yet another case where the researcher has to tear herself away from the computer screen and go to library shelves. There are online sources that make searching for the details of official documents easier, including:

- *UKOP* (*United Kingdom Official Publications*), which is based on the HMSO and Stationery Office listings (1970 onwards) plus a good attempt at listing the non-HMSO publications (1980 onwards); but only available on subscription (*Why?* – it is a commercial service). Or:
- *BOPCRIS* (*British Official Publications Collaborative Reader Information Service*), which is a selection of British parliamentary papers 1801–1995. There is no full text, but it is useful for finding locations if you do not have access to the JISC-sponsored deal. Their website is at:

www.bopcris.ac.uk/bopcris/digbib/home

Box 14   The Case of the Missing Green Paper

In 1998 the Department of Social Security (DSS) published a Green
Paper entitled *New Ambitions for our Country: a New Contract for
Welfare* as part of a series called Command Papers (Green Papers are
consultation documents on UK government policy). In 2006, one of
the authors was asked by a library user to find an online version of
this; not unreasonable given that it was only 8 years old and an
important publication of the early Labour Government years.

The Stationery Office Official Publications site (www.official-
documents.gov.uk) has all Command Papers from May 2005 onwards
and a very few from before then, so there was no point looking there,
as is still the case. Many Command Papers are available online on the
websites of the government department that produced them;
unfortunately the Department of Social Security no longer existed in
2006 as it had been replaced by the Department for Work and
Pensions. Searching the site produced no sign of the document.

The need to see if it was available online elsewhere led to a search
on Google (which has its uses) and plenty of references were found to
it, but not the thing itself. One link led to a referencing guide
produced by the Department of Social Work at the University of
Central Lancashire. In the section on referencing sources obtained via
the Internet they used *New Ambitions for our Country* as an example
and quoted the URL of the document (www.dss.gov.uk/hq/index.htm)
as you are supposed to.[*] Following the link gets a 'Sorry, that page
cannot be found' message on the Department of Work and Pensions
(DWP) site. The DWP had apparently not transferred it from the DSS
site, or had dropped it due to their policy of 'archiving' material for
only two years.

In 2006 that meant there was no online access at all. Off to the
shelves for the print version. Since then the *House of Commons
Parliamentary Papers* database has come along, and there is online
access to all Command Papers back to when they started in 1801. *But*
this is only available, via the special JISC deal, to academic libraries;
you cannot get to it on the Web without using the resource via your
own academic institution.

[*] See Chapter 6 on 'Referencing and Plagiarism'.

Sherlock's stunning discovery – the green paper is missing

Archives

Archives are another category of important resources where there are limitations to what is available online. Archives of business firms, government departments, professional associations, charities and many other organisations are often of vital importance to researchers. They are **primary materials** (or sources), that is, first-hand evidence; they are rarely created with anything else in mind than a specific day-to-day task and they are usually either the only copy of that document or one of very few copies. Even here you should consider *why* the archive document was produced. Factory records of how many widgets[*] were produced and where they were sold during 1967 are less likely to have bias in them than personal letters and diaries, where there might be an eye on an image for posterity; unless, of course, someone at the factory was faking the results to get a bonus.

[*] 'Widget' is used here in the economics and business sense as a hypothetical product. 'Widget' means something very different in computing usage, and, to beer drinkers, it is a device in beer cans to produce bubbles and supposedly make the contents of the can more like draught beer. This is an example of how words can mean many different things, as mentioned in the section on searching bibliographic databases for journal articles.

Only a very tiny portion of this material has been **digitised** to be viewed online by everyone. So the researcher still has to follow the traditional method of actually going to the material she wants. As these are unique documents, popping them in the post to the researcher is not a realistic option. The online world can still help here with directories that describe where archives are held and by giving the researcher descriptions of the material, conditions of use and other details so that she can make a more informed judgement about whether she needs to travel half way round the world.

Even so, most archives are rarely **catalogued** down to individual document level; they just have descriptions of subsections, with a few notes on important items. In practice this would be something like 'Personal Papers'; split up into 'Diaries', 'Correspondence' etc.; and perhaps the correspondence divided up according to the senders or recipients of the letters. Often they don't even have the subsections noted separately, and many collections are completely uncatalogued.

Why are things like this? Because it takes a lot of effort and expense to catalogue, let alone digitise, massive collections of individual items where there is only a very small target audience (the researchers).

Who pays for it? This depends on the material in the archive and who is managing it. For example, transcriptions of the Cabinet Secretary's notebooks are available to download for nothing from the National Archives website because of the Freedom of Information Act. They are transcriptions, rather than a digitisation of the original documents, so that the Cabinet Office could review them for any sensitive information. According to the National Archives website, 'as a by-product of that process the Cabinet Office feels that they may also be useful to researchers' (National Register of Archives, 2009). So, making useful material available to researchers is a 'by-product'. In another part of the National Archives website there is a link to an archive of ships' passenger lists for the late nineteenth and early twentieth centuries, mainly intended to be of use to people tracing their ancestry. The archives are run by 'partner' organisations, ancestry.co.uk and AncestorsOnBoard.com. Searching them is free, but getting a full record and downloading a complete list involves a charge. The '.co.uk' and '.com' parts of the names reveal their commercial origin (as Kipling's' Honest Serving-Men *Who* and *What* would tell you). These organisations have paid the expense of digitising the records because the family history market is such a big one.

Online resources may be able to get you the full document in a limited number of cases, but they are invaluable in providing information about what is held in archives and where those archives are located. The researcher can make a list of the resources she needs to consult before she gets to the archive and can spend the time there using them, without wasting time looking through catalogues based in the archive.

The researcher can also find out if there are any restrictions on access to particular archives and get permission in advance. This is because archives often do not own the material deposited in them, an example being the personal papers of the British Prime Ministers Neville Chamberlain and Sir Anthony Eden, which are in Special Collections at the University of Birmingham, but owned by their descendants. Online sources can also let the researcher know if material is unavailable for any reason, such as conservation work.

The largest and most comprehensive online resources for locating archives are listed in Box 15.

Box 15   Major online resources for locating archives

The **National Register of Archives** contains information about the location of historical records that have been created by individuals, families, businesses and other organisations.

www.nationalarchives.gov.uk/nra/default.asp

Archives Hub contains details of archives in UK universities and colleges.

www.archiveshub.ac.uk/

A2A (Access to Archives) covers local archives in England and Wales.

www.nationalarchives.gov.uk/a2a

Note: if you are going off to use archives, make sure you have a pencil and paper or a laptop with you to make notes; archivists will generally not allow you anywhere near their precious resources with a nasty inky pen.

If you need to use an archive in another country, then the planning and careful consultation of what the archive holds, how you can get your hands on it and the nature of any limitations to access, needs to be sorted out well in advance. For example, to access the East German Secret Police documents, you need to write to the archive months in advance, detailing your project, to gain clearance to visit and view the files you want. A general rule is: the further away the archive, the more pre-planning you need to undertake. Thankfully, nowadays, as we have discussed above, you can check what is available using online catalogues before you set off.

Summary

Remember:

☐ Everything isn't online, or if it is, it may have limitations on its use.

☐ If you follow the advice in this chapter, you will get a lot more out of the online resources you need from libraries and academic sources.

☐ Sometimes the computer has to be put to one side; for example, when you need to look for older statistics in printed volumes, or handle real archives.

And finally ... with any resource, be it printed or online, always remember to:

Evaluate! Evaluate! Evaluate!
(and then Evaluate again).

5 Going it Alone on the Internet

This chapter discusses:

▶ How to evaluate resources on the Internet
▶ How to use search engines
▶ Google
▶ Google Scholar
▶ Wikipedia
▶ Google Books
▶ Your online presence

● Introduction

Many students find it difficult to use the academic resources provided at their college or university, although the authors sincerely hope that the two previous chapters have done much to remove that difficulty. In some cases the student's home institution may not have access to a large range of expensive academic quality online resources. We have already seen some free resources from library and academic backgrounds that are open to all, such as *Intute*, open access publishers and institutional repositories. This chapter will concentrate on other free resources and how to get the best out of them.

When searching the Internet, you have to make sure that you take extra care to evaluate everything. It is important to use only reputable sites where the identity of the author is known (it can be either a person or an

organisation) and where the academic and professional credentials are clear. You don't want to put second-hand or third-hand hearsay into your essays (and your tutor won't, or shouldn't, accept it). The only thing you could do that was worse would be to try to pass it off as your own work (see Chapter 6 on referencing and plagiarism).

Kipling's Six Honest Serving-Men (remember them?) can give a guiding hand here, as in the examples given below.

Box 16   Kipling's Six Honest Serving-Men let loose on the Internet

- **What** is the resource? A report of an academic research project in an online peer-reviewed journal or a newspaper article ('tabloid' or 'broadsheet'?), or a 'blog'?

- **Why** was the resource created? For example, government departmental websites are intended to make information available to the general public; academic level material has to be sifted out by you.

- **When** was the resource created? 'Publication dates' are rare on the Internet, their presence is a good sign. Beware: even sites created by reputable organisations can be out of date, if the funding has run out and they are left to moulder online.

- **How** was the resource created? By extensive/any research or by umpteenth-hand copy and paste? One way to spot this is to read the relevant *Wikipedia* article and see if the same 'fact' or 'opinion' keeps recurring. *Wikipedia* may be fond of copy and paste itself, but it gets repeated ad nauseam elsewhere.

- **Where** was the resource created? A real problem in cyberspace, but a university online repository is better than an anonymous blog posting. Academic sites in the UK have '.ac.uk' in their Internet addresses, whilst American ones have '.edu'. There are also country codes, such as '.de' for Germany (short for 'Deutschland').

- **Who** created the resource? Even if creators are creditable and worthwhile they can have very different viewpoints – for example, HM Prison Service and Nacro (formerly the National Association for the Care and Resettlement of Offenders) on the education of prisoners, even down to the statistics they gather about the subject.

● Search engines

These are mechanised ways of searching the Internet that do not have the human intellectual input of subject gateways. The best known search engine is Google, but there are others including Yahoo! Search, Live Search, Ask.com and Dogpile, which undertakes a combined search of other engines and claims to be 'All the best search engines piled into one'. Whatever search engine you use, you may wish to consider using Mozilla Firefox as your browser of choice, as this attracts less 'malware' (malicious software) than Internet Explorer. Malicious software infiltrates your computer and can, amongst other things, enable other people to track what you are doing, gain personal information and affect your browser settings.

For simple straightforward enquiries such as finding out if an organisation or individual has a website, Google is very useful; much easier than trying to work out the Internet address when these are often inconsistent and unpredictable. For example, note the difference in the following: the Internet address (URL) for the Border and Immigration Agency is:

www.bia.homeoffice.gov.uk

whilst that for the Environment Agency is:

www.environment-agency.gov.uk

However, if you enter some search terms and get several sites, Google provides no help in assessing their value; the 'ranking' used suggests a value judgement, but Google works purely by the number of links and hits to a site, so it may favour popular sites over ones with more intellectual rigour. In effect this is just as arbitrary as the alphabetical listing in printed telephone directories, except that no-one would believe that a company beginning with 'A' gave a better service than one beginning with 'Z'.

Box 17   How to get top ranking in Google
This example of the results of a Google search is included in Tara Brabazon's *The University of Google.* She is critical of Google – and the use of the Internet by students for their research in general – but if her site can be top-ranked for the reasons given (the number of links or hits), just imagine the tricks some unscrupulous people or organisations can use (and do use) to obtain the same result. when 'Tara Brabazon' is entered into Google, the number one returned search is my Home Page, the site developed (by me) to

> promote my career. The links with less hits, but perhaps more
> critical information, are far lower on the ranking. My personal web
> page has so many hits because a link is presented at the bottom of
> each email I send from my work computer. Not surprisingly,
> hundreds of curious undergraduates with a bouncy index finger
> click to their teacher's profile.

(Brabazon, T., 2007: 18)

Another major problem is that the system is entirely automatic and there is no evaluation of the context in which the words you are searching for are used. Words can mean different things in different circumstances and for different academic disciplines. 'Enlargement' is the process by which the former Communist countries of Eastern and Central Europe are being integrated into the European Union. If you put 'enlargement' into Google, you get websites concerned with enlarging all sorts of things that have nothing to do with European political and social integration.

● Google Scholar

Google Scholar makes an effort to target Google's search methods at the student and academic market by excluding commercial sites, those aimed at children, etc. Unfortunately the producers are reluctant to say which sources are included and many major academic publishers are not covered. Google's information about what is included caused one author to comment that 'It reminds me of the informativeness of the communiqués dispensed by the Korean Central News Agency about the nutritional condition in the country' (Jacso, 2005 [unpaginated]). It is equally unclear what dates are covered or how often it is updated. It is clear, however, that there is a definite bias towards science, technology and medicine, rather than social sciences and humanities.

As it retains Google's mechanised indexing there are inconsistencies; to search for Ian Andrew Smith you need to try 'I Smith', 'Ian A Smith', 'Ian Andrew Smith' and 'IA Smith' to make sure you find everything. The examples given for author searching in the Advanced Search suggest that you do not need to include variants that contain full stops, but you cannot be sure of this. Subject searching is even more variable as there are no standard terms used.

Google Scholar's main strength is coverage of free online articles, working papers and reports; when you encounter a source that is fee-based (such as most of the main academic journals), it cannot take you to the full text. You have to go to the subscribed sources at your institution. This may not be obvious, but keep an eye on the top of the page, as the name of your institution appears when you access one of their subscribed sources. In order for this to happen, you need to be either on campus or set up with your institution's off-campus access arrangement (a proxy service). In effect you are not 'going it alone', you are using the resources provided by your library.

Finally, it does not even attempt to locate the websites of important organisations, government departments and professional bodies, which is a feature of subject gateways like *Intute*.

Google Scholar has its uses, but needs to be used alongside other more sophisticated search tools like subject gateways and bibliographic databases. And remember – it is still, after several years, in the Beta (testing) stage – even its creators do not think it is fully functional yet.

Box 18   **If you compare ways of finding information on the Web with the tools you need for an archaeological excavation ...**

Google = a heavy duty excavator shovelling away landfill

Google Scholar = a cute little excavator, with a driver who's trying *very hard* to be sensitive whilst digging

Bibliographic databases and subject gateways = small shovels, trowels and brushes, with all the finds cleaned, bagged and carefully labelled

Based on an idea by Peter Jacso (Jacso, 2005 [unpaginated])

● *Wikipedia*

Wikipedia is a massively popular online encyclopaedia used and abused every day. Many of the criticisms levelled at it are to do with its accuracy and this is obviously a major point to be considered; however, an equally important point about all encyclopaedias (not just *Wikipedia*) is that they are useful secondary, or even more remote, sources – not an end in themselves. They are useful for summarising information and are often useful pointers to more original sources; it is these original sources you have to follow up. In addition you have to use as wide a range of other sources as possible, like the bibliographic databases and subject gateways mentioned above. A piece of university or college-level work that uses solely encyclopaedias is just not good enough, whatever the quality of the works consulted (see Chapter 2 for the recommended number of sources to use in your essay, dissertation etc.).

Traditional print encyclopaedias and dictionaries are space-consuming, and out of date in many areas even before they are printed, so they are a natural for a transfer to online format. The flagship of the encyclopaedic world, the *Encyclopaedia Britannica*, is a subscription-only publication, but the Internet has produced a very popular free rival, *Wikipedia*, that anyone can edit (anyone with access to a computer and the Internet, that is). *Who* is contributing the articles? All are anonymous so no credentials can be checked. *Why* are they contributing – to make information available to all, or from some sinister or just petty malicious purpose, as in the 'Village ridiculed by *Wikipedia* Hijackers' example (see Box 19)? *What* are they contributing – just a copy and paste from elsewhere perhaps? *Wikipedia* and its accuracy have been widely questioned, although in a sense this spotlight does keep them honest and obvious faults are pounced on quickly.

Box 19   Village ridiculed by *Wikipedia* hijackers

'it is best known for having old pubs and brass bands, but Denshaw is also home to cow-shooting, a brothel and a tapeworm epidemic ... if its Wikipedia page is to be believed ...'

'Internet hijackers have posted entries claiming the village has just four people, a problem with obesity and a passion for throwing sheep.'

Metro, 17 April 2008

The online version of the *Metro* article later added some more details:

'The article has since been cleaned up, and locked to changes being made by new or unregistered users.'

www.metro.co.uk/news/article.html?in_article_id=143544&in_page_id=34 (accessed 28/05/08)

In the 15 December 2005 issue of *Nature*, an article went straight to the heart of the matter with a comparison of 42 articles from *Encyclopaedia Britannica* and *Wikipedia* for mistakes and inaccuracies. The articles were 'blind reviewed', so the reviewers did not know the source. The result was that 'the average science entry in *Wikipedia* contained around four inaccuracies; *Britannica* about three' (Giles, 2005: [2]). For the author of the article 'that result might seem surprising' (Giles, 2005: [2]), but the reaction of Encyclopaedia Britannic Inc. was a lot more forceful and the first half of 2006 was occupied with objections by them (Encyclopaedia Britannica Inc., 2006) and responses from *Nature* (Nature, 2006).

This entertaining and thought-provoking row did not really address a major point; in the information-seeking process, encyclopaedias and dictionaries are a beginning, not the final product. They are there for three main purposes:

- To summarise what is available and point you to other more detailed resources, which is something both do, although *Britannica* does so more consistently than *Wikipedia*. Of course, these more detailed sources have to be subjected to Kipling's Six Serving-Men as well.
- To help clarify ideas and formulate search strategies by making you think about what words and concepts *mean* in the academic world; is it the same as what *you* think they mean? Both the works in the *Britannica/Wikipedia* 'head to head' are general ones – it is better to start with specialist works such as the *New Palgrave Dictionary of Economics*, the *International Encyclopaedia of the Social and Behavioural Sciences* or the *Palgrave Literary Dictionary of Chaucer.*
- To find out when terms and expressions came into or out of use. If you are looking into the effect the Structural Funds of the European Union have had you need to know that the term 'Structural Funds' only came into use in 1989 and that a lot of the individual funds were around a lot longer than that. Every subject has its own jargon and 'in' terms and you can waste a lot of time and effort if you ignore this.

Find what is available in your institution, either online or in print, that has this specialised approach. Even if you cannot access something relevant, at least try to check more than one general source; even Britannica says 'we in no way mean to imply that Britannica is error-free; we have never made such a claim' (Encyclopaedia Britannica, 2006: 2).

Box 20   Use the links in *Wikipedia* to gain some context for the information

The *Wikipedia* article on Sakarya University in Turkey contains the following information: 'The city is easy to reach by the help of both buses and trains which are available at any time from other cities. Public buses and other minibus services make it possible for students to get to the campus and other units of the university.'

This is not only dull, but pointless as it has no context in which to evaluate it.

Follow the link in the *Wikipedia* article to the English-language version of the Sakarya University website and you find out that this gem of information is a straight copy and paste from the 'Life at University' section.

Immediately you know *who* is providing the information and you can therefore start to make good guesses at *why* (to attract potential students perhaps?). You can also compare this with similar statements made by your own university or college about how great their facilities are.

To actually find out if this statement is 'accurate' or 'true', you would need to do some extensive research into other resources like Turkish bus and rail timetables, or visit Sakarya University and partake of its transport experience. As this is for purely illustrative purposes, the authors suggest that you don't actually do all this.

http://en.wikipedia.org/wiki/Sakarya_University (accessed 4 July 2008)

www.sakarya.edu.tr/en/?pid=life (accessed 4 July 2008)

Box 21   What *Wikipedia* *is* good for

- If the answer you seek just has to be 'good enough'. For example, one of the authors had a vague memory that August Bank Holiday used to be the first Monday in the month and changed to the last. The Wikipedia article 'Bank holiday' provided confirmation of this and the year when the change happened, 1965 – so the niggling memory was assuaged. However, if you were doing an essay on leisure patterns in the

United Kingdom you would need a great deal more than was contained in this article, although it did provide a start with the mention of the relevant legislation and names to follow up. It also provides an 'External Link' to the Department for Business Enterprise and Regulatory Reform, which offers a more detailed and authoritative summary of the legislation and history of bank holidays, including the August change.

- If you are not using subject gateways and other tools to search the Internet, then *Wikipedia* is at least superior to Google as a search tool, because it actually makes an attempt to distinguish the different meanings of words and acknowledges the fact that several people may have the same name. It proudly uses the 'trying too hard to be impressive' term 'disambiguation' for something that traditional library and academic resources take for granted and have been doing in much more detail for years. Once you find a relevant *Wikipedia* article, there are usually references and external links to other sites, which you can then evaluate using Kipling's Honest Serving-Men. Note that some of the references just lead you back to other parts of Wikipedia. If there are no references and links, then even Wikipedia admits it's a poor effort ('a stub'), and so should you.

- If you do a Google search, read the *Wikipedia* article first, as many of the other things you find in Google will probably have been copied from *Wikipedia*. The time not spent reading the same stuff rehashed over and over again can then be used to do something useful like following up the more valuable links in *Wikipedia*, or even using a more reliable resource mediated by your library.

- Answering quizzes: most of the question compilers will have used *Wikipedia* as their source, so you will get the answers 'right', even if *Wikipedia* is 'wrong'.

Google Books

Google Books has undertaken a massive digitisation scheme at the Bodleian Library in Oxford, which is a copyright deposit library so it has a lot of both scholarly and non-scholarly books. The Bodleian doesn't contain every book published in the UK, but it has a fair-sized chunk of that unobtainable completeness. This project was mainly concerned with nineteenth-century publications as this gets around the problems of copyright in most cases, but even here there are instances of authors who were young when they wrote their first book at the end of the century and lived long enough for them to die well into the twentieth century so that their works are still in copyright and you cannot read the whole thing.

What you are looking for may not be included for all sorts of quirky reasons. In the Oxford Google project, one of these quirky reasons arose from nineteenth-century printing and publishing practices. The usual method of printing a book back then, was to print several pages at a time onto large sheets of paper, fold them into smaller sections and sew the sections together to form the book. It was common practice for publishers not to cut the edges of the pages in each section; the reader was expected to do this with a paper knife as they read the book. Reading a book thus involved a lot of effort, a bit like opening several dozen envelopes. In the Oxford Google project the staff time involved in cutting the pages so that they could be digitally scanned meant that such titles could not be included.

Google Books is still useful to a researcher because it enables her to search even when she does not have the full details of the book's title; Google's fuzzy approach looks for alternatives (as in 'did you mean?').

Media resources

More and more students and scholars are now heading for online media resources instead of reading a newspaper. These so-called 'new' media – the 'new' is generally linked to the manner in which these media are made accessible, online and digitally – is still subject to commercial ownership in a similar fashion to the 'real world' of the printed press. Google itself, of course, is not a free, philanthropic organisation, but a multi-billion-dollar business set on making profit. The online versions of newspapers offer current affairs to readers (surfers) with differing levels of accessibility (to access the full version of the newspaper or magazine usually incurs a charge); the BBC (British Broadcasting Company) offers world news free of charge, which is constantly updated, every few minutes, by its correspondents around the world. The value of such 'immediate' news to students and scholars for their essays and articles is debatable, since such work ought to be a reflection of longer periods of time. However, if you are working on a topical issue, adding some up-to-date case study (of, say, policy towards Iran, or drugs scandals in sport, or MPs' expense claims and democracy) these sites can be of use.

● Your online presence

So far this chapter has been concerned with you finding and using resources that are already available, but you can contribute as well, as long as your efforts meet the Serving-Men's standards.

You can take part in discussion lists, conduct surveys, and email individuals and organisations to obtain extra information. The digital footprint that is created by this activity is like a CV online; according to a JISC-commissioned survey, 68 per cent of employers use search engines to check on candidates (Phipps, 2008 [PowerPoint slide 18]).

However, as the same survey pointed out, there are perils to be avoided. **Dotsam** is a term that has been coined to describe abandoned websites, blogs, wikis, MySpace pages etc., that haven't been updated for ages and yet still remain accessible. The term is modelled on the legal terms 'flotsam and jetsam', which describe the wreckage from a ship; dotsam is wreckage floating around the Internet. Not only does dotsam fail the *When* test, it also raises questions: *Why* is this stuff still hanging around? *What* use is it and *Who* has so little interest in their online persona that they don't tidy it up?

The same survey also emphasised the importance of what it terms the 'Personal vs. Professional' aspects of your online presence. According to this survey, 20 per cent of all employers use 'social networking' sites to run searches on job applicants. The top ten 'turn offs' found in these ranged from 'References to drug abuse' to 'Membership of pointless/silly groups' (Phipps, 2008 [PowerPoint slide 19]). Presumably this is in descending order of heinousness and these two 'turn offs' may well be linked, but it is a reminder that the Internet can bring all sorts of things together that perhaps people might prefer to keep separate.

Another problem you may encounter with your online persona is if you forget how different email communication is compared with face-to-face conversation, where there are all sorts of visual clues as to other people's reactions to what you are saying, and the way you are saying it. If your experience of email has been confined mainly to dealing with people you know, like friends and family, be careful how you phrase your emails, blog postings and the like when dealing with people you do not know. It is quite possible that what seems a light-hearted comment can be seen by some as deeply offensive or insulting – throwing in a smiley-face symbol will not be enough to counteract this.

Over the years a set of norms has emerged to deal with acceptable online behaviour, often called **netiquette**. Examples of this in practice are included in the following sections of this chapter, but one of the most important of the norms is to choose your wording carefully to avoid misunderstandings. Just as important is to check every message before you send it and be sure who you are sending it to. In the early days of email it was common for people to accidentally send personal or confidential messages to everyone on the system. Of course, we are all much more sophisticated these days – that is until we get that sick in the stomach feeling seconds after pressing 'Send'. Out in the harsh world of work, people get fired or face disciplinary action for just this sort of thing, so it pays to get some practice in avoiding it.

Just as with the spoken language, the written language has several different registers. So, when writing to your personal tutor or the convenor of a module you are studying, make sure you are out of the register with which you converse with your peers, as 'yo! send over the module outline. Lol!' is not the appropriate manner in which to address a member of staff. After all, you probably wouldn't address the Vice Chancellor of your university in exactly the same way as you would your peers in the pub – these social conventions translate to the written word and hence, emails, so be aware.

● Emails and email lists

One main use of email for research is to obtain extra detail about something you have read in print or on the Internet, or to obtain clarification about the process involved in, for example, the collection of a particular set of statistics. When composing your email, bear in mind some important points of netiquette. Let the recipient know *who* you are, *why* you want the information and *what* you want to do with the information. The recipient will be judging you with the criteria embodied in Kipling's Serving-Men (who have just, miraculously, reappeared).

Putting something concise and meaningful in the subject box is also useful; if your recipient is swamped with emails every day, blank or vague subjects ('can you help?') make organising and referring to them in their inbox even more difficult. Another way you can help them is by not asking a question that is freely available elsewhere. It will irritate them and make you look a bit foolish if you use 'Contact us' on a website to ask a question that features prominently in the site's FAQ (Frequently Asked Questions) section. Harassing your recipient because you asked the question a day before your paper is due in and they have not replied straightaway is also a pretty major breach of netiquette and says little about your time-management capabilities. If the email is sent to a helpline in, for example, a government department it is likely that they will have response-time targets to meet, but they cannot just drop everything and help you. A private individual has no obligation to respond at all.

Kipling's Honest Serving-Men reappear

Always use a university or college email address, if you have one, for enquiries like this. The '.ac.uk' at the end of this lends more credibility to the enquiry than something like supergirl@hotmail and stands a bigger chance of surviving spam filters. (Note: this email address is thought by the authors to be fictitious, although based on similar examples, but we apologise to anyone who might actually use it.) The institutional address helps to establish *who* you are, as not knowing the identity of correspondents could be a major problem for someone who works in, say, child protection or medical research and is wary about emails from the media and protesters.

As stated earlier, *what* you are going to do with the information is very important – as stated in Chapter 2, an author/academic will usually be pleased to be contacted about their work, but will not want their latest research revealed ahead of time. If they do agree to being quoted, remember to cite and reference them in your finished work. If your institution has a referencing guide, the way to do this may be included in the 'unpublished works' section if you cannot find anything specifically under 'email'. Include the post that they hold, for example Head of Statistics Analysis, to indicate their expertise in the matter and *why* their reply was useful for your work.

Surveys and questionnaires online

If you want to gain information by a survey or questionnaire, email may seem an easy option compared with older methods that involved shoving printed questionnaires into envelopes, or long phone calls. Beware the easy option, it isn't always that easy, as you still have to compose the question-naire and find the right people to send it to. With email there is another problem, as 'response rates to e-mail surveys have declined over the past fifteen years' (Buckler and Dolowitz, 2005: 84). This is largely due to the sheer volume of email which most people receive, added to the fear of viruses in emails from unknown sources. Again, the netiquette rules of making things as easy as possible for the busy people you are contacting apply.

There are ways to use online resources to select people to contact for a questionnaire. *Intute*, with its coverage of government departments and professional and academic organisations, is a good means of finding this information. It also has 'Mailing lists and discussion groups' as one of its resource types, so that you look up a subject like Sociology and find mailing lists for that subject. JISC (Joint Information Systems Committee) maintains large numbers of lists in all academic subjects. The JISCmail National Academic Mailing List Service is at: www.jiscmail.ac.uk/. There will be some overlap in the mailing lists from these two sources, but *Intute* will provide details of non-UK lists. (The astute observer will have noticed that both JISC and *Intute* seem to crop up almost as often as Kipling's Honest Serving-Men. That's because the authors think they are useful to the budding student.)

The mailing lists are intended for researchers in topics as diverse as 'Ageing in Europe' and 'Industrial Relations Research', to pick just two examples at random. You can often see the sort of subjects discussed, to judge whether the list is suitable, by viewing the subject lines in the archive, although it is not possible for people who are not members of the list to read the messages themselves.

Having located suitable lists, from JISC or elsewhere, you then have to contact the list owner to find out their policy on questionnaires from non-members, or if you actually qualify to be a member (the term 'owner' describes a role that includes managing the list and monitoring its content for breaches of copyright and netiquette). With JISCmail lists this can be done by sending an email in the format: [name of list]-request@jiscmail.ac.uk. With other lists you will have to find the contact details yourself, and/or read the terms and conditions about who can use the list.

Once you have the go-ahead to email your questionnaire you need to decide how to send it: as part of the main body of the email or as an attached document. The former has the advantage that the recipient can see straight-away that the survey is brief, easy to answer and relevant – as long as you *have* made it brief, easy to answer and relevant, that is. There may, however, be problems filling in the answers if they involve multiple choice or graded replies, as in ranking the importance of particular factors on a scale of 1 to 5. These problems can be overcome by using web-based survey programs, such as Survey Monkey, which provide you with a ready-made professional survey template (www.surveymonkey.com/). Survey Monkey is free for small-scale surveys; if this is the first survey you have done, keeping the scale of it small is a good idea. The extra effort for the recipient of following a link to the survey is offset by your providing them with something easier to fill in.

● Blogs

In addition to email and mail lists there are other means of discussing various aspects of your subject, such as **blogs**, and news groups. You can keep abreast of new developments and establish a presence online.

The word 'blog' is a contraction of the words 'web' and 'log', with 'log' being used in the sense of a diary of events with a commentary, as with a ship's log (and the Captain's Log in *Star Trek*). Their being web-based makes it possible for many people to add their comments so that it can become a vehicle for online discussions, and there are often links to other sites. Many blogs can be found using Google, and the quality of them may be very low, with unsubstantiated personal opinions and bits copied from *Wikipedia* that are posted by people hiding behind pseudonyms (and therefore providing no *who* to help evaluate their value). *Intute* can be of use here, as 'blogs' is yet another of its resource types, by which you can search the database. It covers blogs originating from both organisations and individuals – for example, the politics blogs include those of the American Academy of Political and Social Science and Jon Snow, the British television newscaster and journalist. *Intute* also includes news groups, but includes them in the 'mailing lists and discussion groups' resource type.

Even if you have been directed to the blog or newsgroup by a reliable source you still need to evaluate it by looking at past postings and the level of the discussion. It is a good idea not to rush in and do your first post without this initial reconnaissance. Reading what is posted without actually contributing is often referred to as 'lurking', which is a very unfortunate term for what is basically common sense and preparation.

Some political blogs have become very influential in the world of politics. For example, the Conservative blogger Guido Fawkes has a huge following and has been linked to breaking news (mostly about resignations in Gordon Brown's government) before the events took place (see: http://order-order.com/).

With blogs and discussion groups the need for netiquette is even greater than in one-to-one emails, as there is the potential to annoy and upset more people. Within a room it is much easier to sense the sharp intakes of breath, the annoyance and exasperation that meet a particularly insulting or stupid comment – although, of course, some individuals may be too thick skinned even to notice that. Bearing in mind that there are many blogs run by politicians, the desire to say something rude and offensive can be very strong, but resist it anyway. Being barred from a blog or a news group does not do anyone's online reputation any good.

Another thing to bear in mind is the confidentiality of information you get from these groups; you might assume, just because people are saying something on the blog, that they are happy to have it repeated elsewhere. They may not have the same sense of their online presence, and how easily traced it is, that the authors of this book are busy fostering in you.

Summary

☐ Online resources not provided by libraries and the academic community may contain valid resources of a sufficiently good quality, but you have to work much harder to find them.

☐ There is an increasing number of free resources that originate from libraries and an academic background; you have to know how to find them.

☐ You can use the Internet to establish your own online presence via emails, questionnaires and blogs, but always be careful to observe the good standards of netiquette.

☐ Your online presence may be of use to you in your future career; or it may not – whilst you are evaluating what's on the Internet, you too are being evaluated.

And finally ... with any resource, be it printed or online, always remember to:

Evaluate! Evaluate! Evaluate!
(and then Evaluate again).

6 Referencing and Plagiarism

All intellectual work at whatever level depends upon us using the ideas and efforts of our predecessors, as expressed in the remark by Sir Isaac Newton: 'If I have seen further [than certain other men] it is by standing upon the shoulders of giants.' (In this case he was referring to the work of his predecessors, Galileo and Kepler.) This is often quoted and it even appears on the edge of the British two pound coin. The following chapter concentrates on how you deal with this debt to the past in your work.

Standing on the shoulders of giants

Pausing only to admire Sir Isaac on the shoulder of a giant and note how many other scholars have said something along the same lines, let us proceed to the rest of this chapter.

Box 22   Some more scholars standing on the shoulders of giants ...

'I say with Didacus Stella, a dwarf standing on the shoulders of a giant may see farther than a giant himself.'

> Robert Burton (1577–1640), *Anatomy of Melancholy*,
> Democritus to the Reader.

'A dwarf on a giant's shoulders sees farther of the two.'

> George Herbert (1593–1633), *Jacula Prudentum*.

'A dwarf sees farther than the giant when he has the giant's shoulders to mount on.'

> Samuel Taylor Coleridge (1772–1834), *The Friend*, sect. i. essay viii.

'Pigmæi gigantum humeris impositi plusquam ipsi gigantes vident' (Pigmies placed on the shoulders of giants see more than the giants themselves).

> Didacus Stella (Diego de Estella) (1524–78), *Lucan*, 10, book Ii.
> John Bartlett, *Familiar Quotations*, 10th edn (1919).

John of Salisbury and Bernard of Chartres (both alive and kicking in the twelfth century) also get dragged into the mix of who first used this expression, but this is enough for you to have got the point that every scholar owes a lot to his or her predecessors or contemporaries and needs to acknowledge this debt.

Referencing

What is referencing

Referencing is the process of informing readers of your work, where you obtained your information, and enabling them to check the sources you used themselves. It also acknowledges your debt to the work done by the authors you have read; you could also have your own work referenced by others.

The actual link in the text of your work that acknowledges your debt is called a **citation**. This points the reader to a complete list of **references**, which are the sources you have referred to in the text. The list usually appears at the end of your work. You may be required to supply a **bibliography**, which is a complete list of the sources you found when doing your research, even if you do not cite them in your finished work. It is an indication of the breadth of your reading and your ability to find resources in an organised and methodical way.

Why you need to reference

There are several good reasons why you need to reference:

- You acknowledge your intellectual debt to other authors upon whose work you have drawn for facts, ideas and opinions. You can also demonstrate the width and depth of your reading and research.
- Whoever reads your work can go back to the original sources and make their own judgements about what you have said, and decide whether they agree with you or not.
- You make clear the distinction between your work and what is in the original, to avoid the suspicion of **plagiarism**. Sloppy record keeping can lead to accidental plagiarism if you get to like a phrase or idea you've read 'somewhere' and start to use it as your own.
- Another important reason for accurate referencing that is less often mentioned is to enable *you* to find the information again. All the record keeping can seem tedious (and, frankly, can be tedious), but it is preferable to having to repeatedly hunt for the same obscure reference – a waste of your effort, a disaster in time management and a source of stress that you do not need.

How to reference

The two main elements for successful referencing are keeping an accurate record of all the books, journal articles, websites and other resources you use and then citing them accurately and consistently in your work using the referencing system approved by your college or university.

You need to find out which referencing system your institution uses; sometimes this can vary between different subject disciplines within the same organisation. The authors of this book use the **Harvard** system of referencing, both throughout the book and in the examples which follow. These are for 'illustrative purposes' only, because there are so many variations and individual styles that you should always use the style recommended by your college or university. Copying the style you see in books and journals will lead to total chaos and confusion, as publishers each have their own house style with its own variations and idiosyncrasies. (Note: the minimal use of citations and references in this book is *not* the style to be copied in your essay. Given the nature of this book, the content of which is drawn from years of the authors' own work and experience in higher education, we are effectively basing most of our advice on our own experience.)

Guidelines are often included in student handbooks, and you could also check to see if your departmental or library website provides referencing guidelines. Often, these are part of a broader 'study skills' or 'academic skills' resource. If your institution does not have a recommended style, you need to consult with your tutor or supervisor as to how you should reference. Consult with them even if there is a recommended style, because they often have their own quirkily personal take on a referencing style.

Keeping Records

You need to keep a record of several elements that go to make up a reference; the basics are listed below. You will see that some of them are the same as Kipling's Serving-Men (who have just cropped up yet again). The author is *Who*, the date is *When*, and so on. This means that whilst you are evaluating your resources you are simultaneously looking at the basic structural elements of your reference – multitasking is great isn't it?

Listed below are the basic elements that have to be recorded, and later in this chapter there are checklists of what you need, to create a proper reference.

- Author: this includes editors, composers, and organisations such as government departments (*Who*).
- Date: date published or created (there may have been delays before something was published) (*When*).
- Title of individual item: for example a book, a book chapter, a journal article, a contribution to a conference, a web page (*What*).
- Where published: includes the physical place a print work is published and the URL (web address) of cyberspace equivalents (ascertain this during your *Where* and *What* questions).
- Publisher: how the work is made available (a combination of *Who* and *What* questions).
- Format: the print or online version, DVD and so on (*What*).
- Version of the source: updated information, new editions and revisions. With web pages this would include the date accessed (*When* and *What*).

- Relevant identifying numbers: volume and issue numbers of a journal, page numbers, number in a series (*Where*).
- Larger work containing your source: the title of the journal that contains an article, the book that includes the individual chapter, the conference that includes an individual paper, or a series of books such as the *Fabian Pamphlets* or the *British Association for American Studies Pamphlets* (*What*).

The only way to get the referencing right is to record the relevant details of all sources consulted as you go along. These details will vary; for example, with web pages you need to record the web address (URL) and date accessed in addition to who wrote the page, etc. For more examples of this, see the section 'Using references in your work' below. Always try to ensure there are at least two copies of your references, on a computer or laptop and on a portable device like a memory stick, so that if one is damaged or lost (or stolen) you always have a backup and do not have to repeat your hard work all over again. If you are using public terminals in a computer cluster you will probably not be able to download to the hard drive, but there will often be an option to save to a network drive which has a designated space for all your work.

Many of the bibliographic databases have the facility to mark articles you consult and put them in a list so that you do not have the problem of getting page and issue numbers etc. wrong. Databases vary, but look out for tick boxes or 'Add to marked list' buttons.

When you photocopy something, write the details on the copy straight-away, if they are not in the part you have copied. Better still, copy the preliminary pages of the book that have all the relevant details. Academic journals often have all the details you want printed on each page; check this is the case with the item you are copying.

Keeping track of all these records can be difficult. Traditionally this was done on index cards kept in boxes, which is time consuming and not very flexible. You also have to be good at filing accurately, and very careful not to drop the box of cards. Copying and pasting the details into a Microsoft Word® document is much quicker, but there is little flexibility in the matter of rearranging the material – you might want to see how many journal articles you have overall, and if you have enough. Also, it is difficult to search, although there is a 'Find' option tucked away in Edit. Microsoft **Excel**® is a better choice as it is possible to reorder the columns and rows in the spreadsheets.

A more sophisticated, although more complicated, alternative is to use **reference management software**, sometimes also called **bibliographic**

software. This has the added benefit that it will format your citations and references for you. See the 'Reference management software' section for more details of this.

Reference management software

Reference management software not only creates a 'database' of your references, but also integrates with word processing to format and insert citations and reference lists into your work as you write it.

There are a number of different packages; you need to see what is 'supported' in your school or college. Reference management software can be Web-based, or come as a separate programme on a CD that you have to purchase. An example of the former is *RefWorks*, where the institution buys the rights to use the package and each user logs in to it the way they would with any other online resource. An advantage is that you do not have to load the software onto the computer you are using to produce your essay or dissertation; you just log in to it.

With other reference software, such as *EndNote*, the software has to be individually loaded onto computers, and in order to use it away from your institution you need to buy your own copy. There are several ways to get details about the resources you have used into your reference manager database. The simplest is just to download direct from the 'marked list' of your choices in a bibliographic database. Commercial factors are at work here; you can download direct from *Web of Science* to *EndNote* because they are both owned by the same company – but it is still essential to check the accuracy of what results from this process. If you want to transfer bibliographic data to *EndNote* from, say, *Sociological Abstracts*, you need a little extra piece of software called a 'filter'. Sometimes it is not possible to download at all, because your source does not have the necessary computer tagging to indicate things like titles and authors – these are needed to match up with the equivalent tags in the reference management software. In this case you have to type or cut and paste into an online form.

Using references in your work

The following section gives some examples of citations and references in the Harvard, or Author–Date, system of referencing. At the end is a brief note about an alternative system called, variously, 'Numeric', 'Numbering', 'Humanities' or 'Vancouver' that you may encounter.

Please note that the examples of how to format citations and references given here are 'for illustrative purposes only', to demonstrate the basic principles. Always refer to any manuals or guides on referencing produced by your institution for their preferred style.

CHECKLIST

Checklist of details you need for **Books**

- Name of the author(s)
- Name of the editor(s)
- Year of publication
- Title of the book
- Chapter title, if the book is a collected work
- Edition (if it is not the first edition)
- Place of publication
- Publisher
- Page numbers (these are for the in-text citations only, not the reference)

The in-text citation for a book uses the author's family name, the year of publication and in many cases a page number, although the layout varies according to what is in the text. If you mention the author's name in your work, the citation will look like this:

Bloggs (1990) demonstrated the importance of close family ties in such societies ...

If the family name does not occur naturally within the text the result is:

These ideas have been countered by other specialists in the field (Graf, 1994; Brown, 2000).

When referring to a specific point, such as the source of a quotation or a particular statistic, page numbers are also included:

Ash (2008: 318), when reviewing the history of European unification, takes the view that 'The attempt at European unification since 1945 thus stands out from all earlier attempts by being both peaceful and implemented.'

The reference, usually listed at the end of an essay etc., starts off with the details in the citation (but without any page numbers) and then has the title of the book, the place of publication and the publisher, like this:

Alcock, P. (1993) *Understanding Poverty*. Basingstoke: Macmillan.

The title of the book is emphasised by italics or bold type, as this information is the best starting point for tracing the book. This is the first edition of this book; if you are using later editions which may contain updated facts, revised theories and extra items in the bibliography you have to indicate this by including the edition number and the year of publication.

Alcock, P. (1997) *Understanding Poverty*, 2nd edn. Basingstoke: Macmillan.

The edition is usually clearly indicated on the cover of the book, the title page and so on (a new edition is a useful selling point), although sometimes it is just described as 'Revised' without a number, which is how you would have to describe it in the reference. Ignore any dates in the book that refer to 'impressions'; these are just reprints, with an unaltered text.

If there are two authors then you include both in the citation and in the reference:

Spooner, C. and McEvoy, E. (2007) *The Routledge Companion to the Gothic*. Abingdon: Routledge.

Or:

Janoski, T. and Hicks, A. M. (1994) *The Comparative Political Economy of the Welfare State*. Cambridge: Cambridge University Press.

For three or more authors the usual convention is to give the first, followed by the abbreviation 'et al.' which stands for the Latin phrase *et alia*, 'and others'.

'Author' can also mean what is called a corporate or organisational author, like the British Broadcasting Corporation, which you can use in citations and references if there is no named personal author. If you still cannot find an author you can use the title of the book in the citation and the reference, like this:

Dod's Parliamentary Companion (1992) 173rd edn. Etchingham: Dod's Parliamentary Companion.

You may want to refer to a chapter within a book; the structure of the reference will depend on whether or not the author of the chapter is also responsible for the whole book. If the author of the chapter is also the editor of the book then the reference will look like this:

Parrot, B. (1990) *The Dynamics of Soviet Defense Policy*. Washington DC: Wilson Center Press, pp. 7–40.

When the author of the chapter is not the editor of the book the reference looks like this:

> Hancock, S. (2005) 'Fantasy, Psychology and Feminism: Jungian Readings of Classic British Fantasy Fiction'. In Reynolds, K. (ed.) *Modern Children's Literature*. Basingstoke: Palgrave Macmillan, pp. 42–57.

Or:

> Lake, D. (1991) 'British and American Hegemony Compared: Lessons for the Current Era of Decline'. In Fry, M. G. (ed.) *History, the White House and the Kremlin*. London: Pinter, pp. 106–122.

This makes it clear that the chapter by Lake in the collection edited by Fry has been drawn upon specifically, rather than the book as a whole.

The examples above do not cover every eventuality; but they do provide the basic underlying principles. Most institutions have their own referencing guides which go into much more detail and also provide guidance about their own preferred style (does it use 'and' or '&' to link the names of two authors?). Find out what is in use where you are before you start writing and referencing, not after.

CHECKLIST

Checklist of details you need for **Journals** – many journals have details such as the journal name, volume and issue numbers, and date printed across every page.

- Name of the author(s)
- Title of the article
- Title of the journal
- Volume and/or issue number
- Page numbers of the journal article (these appear in the citation and the reference)

For a journal that is only available online and has no print equivalent you also need:

- The Internet address/URL
- The date you accessed the site

The in-text citation for a journal article follows the same layout as for books. The full reference for the journal article uses the details in the checklist in the order shown in this example.

Riggio, E. (2002) 'Child Friendly Cities: Good Governance in the Best Interests of the Child'. *Environment and Urbanization*, 14 (2), pp. 45–58.

The reference starts off with the same details as the citation and then has the title of the article, the journal in which it appeared and the volume number, issue number and pages, which enable you to locate the article within the journal. In this case it is the title of the *journal* that is emphasised by italics or bold type, as this information is the best starting point for tracing the article, either in print or online. In some versions of Harvard the page numbers are indicated by a colon (**:**). By the way, 'pp' is not a misprint, it is a convention used to refer to the plural word 'pages', if the article was one page long then you use just 'p'.

If you are using the online version of a printed journal you can use the same layout. However, if the journal is online only, then extra details have to be added to indicate that it is online, plus the Internet address and the date accessed.

Bailey, S. (2005) 'Assessing the Impact of the Freedom of Information Act on the FE and HE Sectors'. *Ariadne* [online], 42.
Available from: www.ariadne.ac.uk/issue42/bailey/ [Accessed 20 June 2005].

The URL is usually not underlined in the reference; the underlining obscures the underscore symbol (_) often used in URLs. When Microsoft Word® does the underlining automatically after you cut and paste the URL you can click on 'Edit' and 'Undo AutoFormat' to remove it.

CHECKLIST

Checklist of details you need for **websites**:

- Name of the author(s)
- Title of the website
- Date the website was created or last updated
- The Internet address/URL
- Date you accessed the site

Citing and referencing for online resources such as websites follows the same principles as for print resources, but extra details have to be added in line with their own special characteristics. In the UK the basic principles of citing and referencing are based on British Standards, the most recent of which is BS 5605, which was published in 1990, and a lot has happened online since then.

The following example is one attempt to combine the basic details shared with print media with those needed to trace something online. The in-text citation is easier because it does not need all the extra online details; it is just pointing you to the full reference:

(Centre for Advancement of Women in Politics, 2008).

The full reference has the corporate author first, followed by the date when the information was last updated and then the title of the web page. The [Online] note is not included in all referencing systems. The main new features follow next; the URL (Internet address) and the date you accessed the site.

Centre for Advancement of Women in Politics (2008). *Women Members of the House of Commons* [Online].
www.qub.ac.uk/cawp/UKhtmls/MPs2005.htm
[Accessed 6 February 2009].

As with journals online, the URL is usually not underlined in the reference; the underlining obscures the underscore symbol (_) often used in URLs. When Word does the underlining automatically after you cut and paste the URL you can click on 'Edit' and 'Undo AutoFormat' to remove it.

The variations in layout between institutions for non-traditional media are even greater than for print, so it is important to check up on local practice. Websites are the major problem, but there are also instances where you might have to reference things as diverse as emails sent to you containing useful information, videos, films, broadcasts and even recordings of interviews you have conducted. If your local guidance does not cover a specific example you can look at what other institutions do that could be adapted. A lot of referencing guides produced by universities and colleges are available online. Putting 'Harvard referencing system' into Google is a useful way of tracking these down. The results of such a search are easy to evaluate; the large number of .ac.uk sites all tell you *Who* is providing the information, and the *Why* is also clear – to help students like you.

The alternative **Numbering** system contains the same elements as Harvard, but uses numbers for the citations, which refer you to a references list that may appear as footnotes, or at the end of the chapter, or of the whole work.

The citations appear in the text like this:

Parkinson's disease is a degenerative disease of the basal ganglia of the brain, characterised by muscular rigidity, tremor, and a shuffling gait (1). It was first described in 1817 by James Parkinson, after whom the condition was later named (2).

The citations lead to a reference list like this:

1. Walton, J., Barondess, J. A., Lock, S., editors. *The Oxford Medical Companion*. Oxford: Oxford University Press, 1994.
2. Parkinson, J. An essay on the shaking palsy. London: Whittingham and Rowland, 1817.

● Plagiarism

What is plagiarism?

The word 'plagiarism' derives from the Latin for kidnapper, but as a crime it is really closer to a mixture of theft and fraud; the theft of someone's ideas, which are then passed off as the plagiariser's own efforts (see Grix, 2010).

The most basic form of plagiarism is copying chunks of text without quotation marks or any acknowledgement in the form of citations and references. Copying and pasting from the Internet is a favourite way of doing this, as there are now lots of research papers online so that you can cut and paste something a bit classier than *Wikipedia*. Making minor amendments to the text is in some senses even worse, as it implies more active dishonesty, rather than just laziness. It is not just text that can be plagiarised: unacknowledged ideas, diagrams, tables and pictures also count as plagiarism.

Rephrasing the original in your own words is still plagiarism if no acknowledgement is given to the original source. This is because plagiarism is not just copying words, it is just as much about copying ideas and theories without due acknowledgement. **Paraphrasing** is the process of summarising another's ideas in your own words, and if done properly it is a perfectly acceptable academic practice. See the 'How to avoid plagiarism' section for examples of how to paraphrase properly.

If a student submits the same piece of work for two, or more, assignments this counts as **self-plagiarism**. No-one else's work is being copied (unless there was plagiarism in the first outing of the work), but it is still dishonest. It is permissible to quote yourself, which may seem a little bizarre at first, but it is a good way to demonstrate the extent to which your opinions and understanding have progressed since the original work (if they have not progressed, it would be a good idea not to draw attention to the fact). You

The internet has made cutting and pasting much easier

are also not allowed to submit the same work to two different institutions. One of the authors had the interesting experience of being presented with a piece of work for an MA module registering a 98 per cent similarity rate on plagiarism-detecting software (this is the equivalent of a complete copy and paste job). The piece in question turned out to be from an MA submitted by the student the year previously to a different university (for more about plagiarism-detecting software, see below in this chapter).

Why you need to avoid plagiarism

There are at least three main groups of people who will not appreciate plagiarism: your tutors and supervisors, your fellow students, and employers and colleagues in the world of work after you leave the world of academe. (And of course, the authors of the works you plagiarise will not be pleased either!)

Academic supervisors and tutors in higher and further education are trying to help students and enable them to find things out, and also to think and reason for themselves, which is the main point of education. A student who does no 'finding out' other than looking up something on *Wikipedia* and no more thinking and reasoning than cutting and pasting it into their work is a complete negation of this. It is also an insult to the supervisor's intelligence to think they would be fooled by something like this. It is not unknown for students to plagiarise their own supervisor's work in essays they hand in, which adds outright stupidity to the original offence.

Fellow students will not like plagiarists either, especially if they are the ones being plagiarised by having their work copied. Even if there is no direct copying, it is not pleasant for students who have made some effort in their work to then see others trying to fake their way through. Insulting the intelligence of the tutor and the work effort of fellow students is not a particularly edifying double whammy.

In a JISC (the Joint Information Systems Committee) commissioned survey, PhD students were asked what they disliked about the work of fellow students in online research. One of the replies was 'Plagiarism, if something is on your site and is not referenced appropriately or due credit given, you may attract an accusation of plagiarism' (Phipps, 2008 [PowerPoint slide 20]).

It is not just a case of academia being awkward and stuffy; out in the world of work, employers and colleagues are not going to be fans of plagiarism either. Work colleagues are going to be at least as annoyed as fellow students at having their ideas copied and claimed by the plagiariser.

As for the employer's view of plagiarism, we only have to look to the high-profile case of Dr Raj Persaud, a consultant psychiatrist and broadcaster. In 2006, King's College London issued a statement regarding plagiarism allegations involving him and he had to withdraw from his 'honorary position' at the Institute of Psychiatry (King's College London, 2006 [unpaginated]). It can safely be said that employers do not like having to issue statements about allegations made against anyone associated with them, and they also do not like the attendant bad publicity. Dr Persaud's situation worsened in 2008 when he appeared before the General Medical Council's Fitness to Practice Panel after accusations that he had copied the work of others in a book and some articles. He was suspended for three months, but not 'struck off' the GMC register completely because 'there had been no patient harm, that his plagiarism was not financially motivated, that it did not relate to research fraud and that it was unlikely to be repeated' (Jenkins, 2008 [unpaginated]). This was in June; when the three-month suspension ended he did not return to his consultant's job, which he had held for twelve years (Sturcke and Wainwright, 2008 [unpaginated]).

Plagiarism-detecting software

If anyone still doubts the gravity of plagiarism and the efforts being made to combat it, they need only point their browser to the JISC Plagiarism Advisory Service website at: www.jiscpas.ac.uk/. JISC promotes the use of technology in higher and further education within the UK. One particular piece of technology they promote very heavily is Turnitin, an electronic plagiarism-detection service.

Turnitin is used by over 80 per cent of UK universities (as of late 2008) and also in colleges and by professional bodies. The text of an essay or dissertation is submitted to Turnitin, which then checks it against a database of online resources such as newspapers and journals, online essay banks and even previously submitted work by the same student (self-plagiarism is still plagiarism). Turnitin then produces an 'Originality Report' based on these comparisons. Copying and pasting is quick and simple, but it leaves an easily identifiable trail. Most academics can detect the point in an essay where the lumbering prose of the writer suddenly becomes concise, lucid and insightful, and then just as suddenly lapses back – now it is easier to trace the origins of the suspiciously good bits. Students attempting to smooth over this transition by adding a few of their own words or by replacing words should take heed that Turnitin highlights these changes in a different colour and seals the fate of the plagiariser, as this is a clear example of the *intent* to deceive and would lead to disciplinary procedures and, at worst, to expulsion from the student's place of learning.

Plagiarise? ... Many eyes see what you do

How to avoid plagiarism

In order to avoid plagiarism it is necessary to maintain a firm distinction between your own opinions and thoughts and the opinions and thoughts of the authors in your sources. Referencing and citing properly enable you to indicate the work of others and to give credit where it is due. There are other techniques with which you can combat the slide into accidental plagiarism: it is important to know how to use **quotations** from your sources and how to summarise someone else's opinions by paraphrasing. These two skills are discussed in this section. In addition, it is important to avoid the temptation of a quick-fix approach when under pressure from deadlines, and include some cut and paste in your work, so this section concludes with a word or two about **time management**.

A major way of avoiding plagiarism is to try to use your own words as much as possible at all stages. When making notes, try to avoid copying too much from your sources and, if you do copy, make sure you indicate that it is the original text. If you use your own words in notes you get to understand what you are reading at a deeper level; you will not just be recording facts to be memorised and regurgitated later. Understanding more, and at the same time diminishing the chances of even accidental plagiarism, is pretty useful multitasking (to repeat a point already made at the end of Chapter 2).

If you do use quotations, use them sparingly, to illustrate a major point, or as an example of what you consider the 'typical' point of view of a particular class or social group. Try to decide if something is a 'good quote' as you make notes. An essay where a large portion of the text is made up of quotations is unlikely to gain high marks, even if you cite and reference correctly, because there will be so little of your own thought in it.

When quoting, use quotation marks to indicate anything from another source, with longer quotations indented and separated from the rest of the text, as in these examples based on the following piece of text taken from *History of the Present* by Timothy Garton Ash.

> The attempt at European unification since 1945 thus stands out from all earlier attempts by being both peaceful and implemented. An idealistic interpretation of this historical abnormality is that we Europeans have at last learned from history. The 'European civil war' of 1914 to 1945 – the second and still bloodier Thirty Years War – finally brought us to our senses.

This is an example of a short quotation in quotation marks:

Ash (2008: 318), when reviewing the history of European unification, takes the view that 'The attempt at European unification since 1945 thus stands out from all earlier attempts by being both peaceful and implemented.'

For a longer quote, you use indentation and separate the quote from the rest of the text, without quotation marks:

Ash (2008: 318), when reviewing the history of European unification, takes the view that:

> The attempt at European unification since 1945 thus stands out from all earlier attempts by being both peaceful and implemented. An idealistic interpretation of this historical abnormality is that we Europeans have at last learned from history. The 'European civil war' of 1914 to 1945 – the second and still bloodier Thirty Years War – finally brought us to our senses.

You can remove words from quotations if they are very long, or if the relevant part begins partway through a sentence. All words cut out need to be indicated by an ellipsis, which is a fancy name for three full stops ... However, be careful with this: if the quotation is so long that it needs chunks cut out of it, why are you using so much in the first place? It is better to extract and use the really relevant bits. There is also a danger of misrepresenting the original. If a theatre critic reviews a play with the words 'this production has a complete absence of passion, originality and good old fashioned stagecraft' and the theatre puts up a poster outside with 'this production has ... passion, originality and good old fashioned stagecraft' that might be amusing, but it would also be dishonest. It is likely that a tutor's reaction to similar misrepresentation in an essay would cut out the stage of being amused and go straight to annoyance at the dishonesty.

Extra words can also be inserted to clarify the quotation, but again they have to be clearly indicated, usually by enclosing additions within square brackets [ ]. It might be worth considering how useful a quote is if it needs extra help from you, but it is often necessary to clarify a point when quoting the exact words of interviewees. For example: 'Throughout the entire famine they [the central government] gave us no help at all.'

Paraphrasing is another way of expressing the ideas and opinions in the sources you read, using your own words. However, it must be done properly, with correct citations and referencing. This is demonstrated in the two examples of paraphrasing in the 'Proper paraphrasing' box (Box 23).

Please note that whilst acceptable paraphrasing of others' ideas is good in itself, students need to critically evaluate these ideas and have their own opinions as well.

Box 23   Proper paraphrasing

Here is the original extract from a book, and two paraphrased versions of it.

This is the original extract from *History of the Present* by Timothy Garton Ash:

> The attempt at European unification since 1945 thus stands out from all earlier attempts by being both peaceful and implemented. An idealistic interpretation of this historical abnormality is that we Europeans have at last learned from history. The 'European civil war' of 1914 to 1945 – the second and still bloodier Thirty Years War – finally brought us to our senses.

Paraphrase A

The attempt at European unification since 1945 is different from all earlier attempts as it is peaceful and has actually taken place. An idealistic interpretation of this is that Europeans have at last learned from history. They were brought to their senses by the European civil war of 1914 to 1945.

Reference:
Ash, T. G. (2000) *History of the Present.* Updated edn. London: Penguin Books.

Paraphrase B

Ash (2000) suggests that an 'idealistic' view of the progress of European unification since 1945 is that Europeans do not want to repeat the bloodshed of the major European wars of the twentieth century and earlier.

Reference:
Ash, T. G. (2000) *History of the Present.* Updated edn. London: Penguin Books.

The difference between them can be summed up thus:

Paraphrase A

This is unacceptable paraphrasing. Large parts of it have been copied straight from the original text, without quotations or any in-text citation. There is therefore no way to know that this is Timothy Garton Ash's view – the 'reference' at the end is just free floating with no connection to the rest of the essay.

Paraphrase B

This is acceptable paraphrasing. There is a citation directing the reader to the source of the opinion and it has been largely rephrased in different words, although by the nature of the topic, 1945, European, etc. have cropped up again. The quotation marks around 'idealistic' help to indicate that this is Timothy Garton Ash's own assessment of this view.

If you are under pressure to get several things done, with lots of dead-lines looming, it can be tempting to copy and paste text into an essay or dissertation to pad it out. If the resulting effort is rejected because it is plagiarised, the consequences are usually worse than getting low marks for a poor effort that is at least honest. The resulting black mark on your record and the need to re-do the work will add even more to the stress. There are different levels of plagiarism, ranging from the outright attempt to deceive, which should see the candidate expelled from their institution for a larger piece of work, to cases of sloppy referencing, which should result in a warning. If you are careful with your note-taking and recording of the details of the material you read, you should not have any worries in this area.

Good time management can help you plan ahead and try to smooth out the crisis points. Universities and colleges are well aware of the demands on students' time, with increasing numbers working part time to pay fees. Many now offer advice on time management and dealing with other pressures; check to see what is available at your institution. Remember to see what help your local students' union can offer as well.

In addition to this, the University of Middlesex has compiled a list of tips on time management that are from actual, real students, rather than from academics or librarians:

www.mdx.ac.uk/www/study/Timetips.htm

Further reading: courses and quizzes about plagiarism

There are a number of interactive courses and quizzes which will help you to understand and avoid plagiarism by explaining the basic principles and giving plenty of practical examples. If your institution has one of these it will certainly be drawn to your attention when plagiarism features in your induction. If it does not, or you have not started yet, then there are some freely available tutorials and quizzes listed below. Note the wide geographical range of originating universities in this listing, an indication that plagiarism is a major concern for all academic institutions:

Empire State College (State University of New York) – Plagiarism quiz:

www.esc.edu/ESConline/Across_ESC/library.nsf/wholeshortlinks2/
Plagiarism+Quiz?opendocument

This needs a Flash plugin to view it.

Monash University – Plagiarism tutorial:

www.lib.monash.edu.au/tutorials/citing/plagiarism.htm

This needs a Flash plugin to view it.

University of Prince Edward Island – Plagiarism tutorial:

www2.upei.ca/library/plagiarism/

The University of Princeton places its plagiarism pages firmly in the 'Academic Integrity' section of its website:

www.princeton.edu/pr/pub/integrity/08/intro/index.htm

● Copyright

You may be vaguely aware of **copyright** as something to do with the © symbol that appears on books and DVDs, but as a student it will have greater implications for you. Copyright is intended to give authors control of the work they produce and also provide payment to them as encouragement to create new works and contribute to research and learning. The legal position is that these works are their **intellectual property** and stealing and using the author's ideas is just as illegal as stealing a piece of physical property like a book from a shop or library. We have already come across plagiarism, which is passing off someone else's work as your own; copyright deals with stealing extra copies of the work and avoiding payment to the originator.

Copyright gives the original author, or their publisher, exclusive rights for the publication, distribution and adaptation of the works, and often the authors of an adaptation have rights as well. Intellectual property is like any other form of property in that rights can be passed on to the author's heirs and so works can be 'in copyright' for several years after an author's death. This period varies with the legislation of the country where the works are published; currently the UK has a seventy-year rule. When this time is up, the work is then 'out of copyright' or 'in the public domain'. You will notice the results of this when using Google Books, where older books can be freely downloaded in full, whilst more recent ones only have brief extracts available without payment.

Fortunately for the student, there are exceptions to the completely rigid enforcement of copyright that are intended to encourage the spread of ideas and knowledge within the academic world. These are known in the UK legislation as 'fair dealing' and are included in the Copyright Designs and Patents Act 1988 and the Copyright and Related Rights Regulations 2003. In case you do not have the time to read these in detail, the following sections give you a brief view of what they mean to you.

Fair dealing allows the use of acknowledged quotations of the work in reviews, academic essays, dissertations and theses without having to ask the author's permission. Note that 'acknowledged' involves quoting, paraphrasing and referencing correctly. Outside academia, where there are commercial forces at work, this dispensation does not apply; apart from quotations used in reviews (all authors want as much publicity from reviews as possible).

Fair dealing also extends to the amount an individual can photocopy for their own private study. The photocopiers in your institution will have notices next to them suggesting the acceptable limits of what you can copy, which is usually something like this:

- One complete chapter, or up to 5% of a long book (whichever is the greater).
- One article from a single issue of a journal.
- Up to 10% of a short book (one without chapters) but not exceeding 20 pages, and the same for a report or a pamphlet.
- There will also be a warning that the number of images, photographs, graphs and so on that can be copied is also restricted.

It is important to stress that this is for one copy for your own use. Publishers also have the right to impose stricter rules on their own publications, regardless of more general established practice. Broadly speaking, the same practice applies to how much you can download, although again publishers can impose their own restrictions, as with some eBooks, which only allow five pages of the original text. It is also much easier for publishers of online materials to detect if users are downloading too many articles from a single issue of a journal.

Another example of how copyright considerations affect online materials is with inter-library loans from the British Library; online access is rapidly replacing paper copies in this area. If your library gets you an inter-library loan of a journal article that they do not have in electronic form, you can only access the article once, so you have to print it out straightaway.

A more recent development in fair dealing concerns making copies that are more accessible to the visually impaired. This includes things like enlarging the print or making the work available in electronic format that can be

Go easy on the photocopying

* = Copyright Licensing Agency

read using special software. The Copyright (Visually Impaired Persons) Act 2002 does impose limitations. There must not be an existing alternative (for example, an eBook version of the print copy), and the copying has to be done from an item that the visually impaired person has a right to use, like their own copy or a copy already in the library where they are registered. There is also an exception to the 'for your own use' requirement, in that the copying can be done for the person if their impairment is sufficiently great that they cannot do it for themselves.

Copyright law still tends to be rooted in the print era, but recently **'Creative Commons' licences** have been developed, where authors grant some rights to the public to access their work online. These rights can vary in the amount of access they permit and the purposes for which the work can be used. If you have not come across these before, a major example in the non-academic world can be found in the Flickr photo-sharing site. These more flexible approaches to copyright are also reflected in the **Open Access** movement, with the many university and other sites mentioned in Chapter 4 that provide access to academic resources.

Summary

☐ Always acknowledge the ideas and efforts of other people.

☐ Start collecting the details of the material you read, from day one.

☐ Never copy someone else's work or try to pass it off as your own – plagiarism is dishonest and can have serious consequences when discovered.

☐ To keep a clear distinction between your work and that of other people, use referencing, paraphrasing and clearly acknowledged quotations.

☐ Be aware of how copyright laws affect what you can photocopy and download.

Summary of Concluding Points

It is difficult to offer a traditional conclusion to this slim volume, principally because we do not have one, central argument running throughout the book that we want to hammer home; rather we have a number of tips and points about gathering information for research. However, some concluding points pick out the key features and main messages of the preceding chapters:

- Familiarise yourself with the language research is conducted in; learn the generic terms and those specific to your academic discipline. Do not be put off by long words and people who spout them – learn the -isms and -ologies of research and the role they play.
- When undertaking a literature review, attempt to pick out patterns, groups or types of literature with which you can structure your work. Which research methods do scholars use? What is their focus, individuals or institutions? Although such divisions may appear artificial, without them you will not grasp the literature around a certain topic. Of equal importance is the fact that you will not be able to inform the reader where your project fits in with the literature around your topic.
- Always evaluate every resource you use, regardless of whether it is print or online or whether it comes from the library or the World Wide Web. Evaluation is an important skill in both academia and the world of work.
- The online resources provided by libraries and the academic community have been developed over many years to make them suitable for the task of creating valid academic work. Take full advantage of them by making sure you know how to gain access to the online journals and books at your university or college. Open access sources will enable you to gain free access to resources at other institutions as well.
- Online resources not provided by libraries and the academic community may contain valid resources of a sufficiently good quality, but you have to work much harder to find them and eliminate the dross.

- You need to be aware that everything is not online, or if it is, it may have limitations on its use. At some point you have to leave your computer, for example to look for older statistics in printed volumes, or handle real archives. This can bring you closer to the realities of your subject.
- In addition to using the Internet to find resources, you can use the Internet to establish your own online presence via emails, questionnaires and online discussions. This online presence may be of use to you in your future career; or it may not, if you ignore netiquette and offend people.
- In your work, always acknowledge the ideas and efforts of other people. Never copy someone else's work or try to pass it off as your own – plagiarism is dishonest and can have serious consequences when discovered.
- To keep a clear distinction between your work and that of other people, use referencing, paraphrasing and clearly acknowledged quotations. If you collect the necessary details as you go along it is much easier to remember what are your own ideas and opinions, and those you have read.

And finally ... with any resource, be it printed or online, always remember to:

**Evaluate! Evaluate! Evaluate!
(and then Evaluate again).**

Part III

Glossary

Glossary

The following glossary of terms lists the words marked in bold throughout the main text. Most of these words are either explained in the main text or their meanings are obvious from the context in which they have been used. The best idea is to look at both the glossary *and* the word or term in the text, to get a better understanding of it. Highlighted terms in the glossary are for cross-reference purposes.

Abstracts
In Chapter 2 we suggested using abstracts as part of the 'skimming' technique in your literature search/review. An abstract is a summary of the content of a journal article, a conference paper or any other publication. They are used in **bibliographic databases** to help researchers decide if the items they have found in a search are relevant to their research. One especially useful way of doing this is to highlight within the abstract the search terms used by the researcher.

Abstracts are important as aids to sifting through the enormous amount of results that online searching can produce, and can help save on downloading time, printing costs and the costs of obtaining an item from another library that turns out to be irrelevant.

Approach
An approach describes the method used or steps taken in setting about a task or problem, especially with reference to which means of access or which sources are to be employed. Approaches are, like **methodologies**, particular ways of producing or getting at knowledge and, as such, are very much dependent on the view of the world taken by those who use them, or to put it in academic language, they are informed by the paradigmatic assumptions upon which they are based. For example, a neo-liberal approach to the way in which the world financial system works is underpinned by specific **ontological** and **epistemological** assumptions which would not necessarily be shared by other approaches to the same subject of enquiry in the same field. Given the so-called 'credit crunch' in recent

years, we could suggest that this 'approach' is likely to be challenged by another. Confusion arises when academics use the term 'approaches' to mean specific disciplinary 'perspectives', specific **theories** and research **paradigms**.

Athens

This is a system which enables you to use just one username and password to prove that you have the right to use several databases, so that you do not have to remember several different passwords. In the Summer of 2008, Athens ceased to be the major means of authenticating rights of access and was replaced by a new system called **Shibboleth**. Athens continues in use for some databases until they can be made compliant with the new system. A widely held misconception about Athens is that it provided databases; in fact it only gave you access rights to resources coming from a wide range of publishers and suppliers. Do not be confused by people telling you 'It used to be on Athens, I don't know where it is now.' In most cases 'it' is where it has always been, you just use a different procedure to get to it.

Author–Date

Another name for the **Harvard** referencing style, so called because the **citations** within the text include the author and publication date of the work cited.

Bibliographic databases

'Bibliographic' is the term used to describe all the details of a published work, such as author, date, title, publication year, page number etc., that enable you to trace it, use it and provide **references** for others to locate it. The term has also been extended to cover useful details for non-print resources, such as DVD running times or formats. Bibliographic databases are online versions of the old printed **indexes**, providing you with the bibliographic details of works on your subject. It is often possible for them to take you to the full text of what you want online as well. Bibliographic databases often have **abstracts**, which summarise the works found to help you decide how relevant they are to your research. Most now also have alerting services that help keep you up to date with new publications in your area of research.

Bibliographic software

Software that you can use to record the bibliographic details of the resources you consult and use in your work. A more common name is the rather catchy '**reference-management software**'.

Bibliography

A listing of resources on a subject, giving all the details needed to locate those resources – author, title, the date published and so on. Bibliographies can vary in scale and scope from massive databases such as the *International Bibliography of the Social Sciences* to a list at the end of a student's extended essay of what they have found whilst working on the essay. In Chapter 2, we offer some guidelines on how many sources your bibliography ought to contain. In general, the more the merrier, so long as they are recognisable as reputable sources. Needless to say, an essay without an adequate bibliography of such sources is certain to attract low marks.

Blogs

'Blog' is a contraction of the words 'Web Log', with the word 'log' being used in the sense of a diary of events with a commentary, as with a ship's log (and the Captain's Log in *Star Trek*). Because the blog is web-based it is possible for many people to add their comments so that it can become a vehicle for online discussions. The quality of the discussion can often be very low, being little more than unsubstantiated ramblings by individuals about their life (or lack of a life). Blogs of this low standard often turn up in Google searches, but it is possible to locate blogs of academic value using *Intute.* In this you can limit searches by 'Resource type', a drop-down listing of things like government publications and bibliographic databases – and increasingly blogs appear in this listing as well.

Case study

Case studies are a very popular way of structuring projects. A case study is a restriction or narrowing of focus to one or more towns, individuals, organisations, etc., which are studied in detail. Usually a variety of **quantitative** and **qualitative research** methods are used within case-study approaches, with the aim of shedding light on the object of study. Case studies represent particular strategies for research, involving investigation of a particular contemporary phenomenon within its real-life context, and employing multiple sources of evidence.

Catalogue

A catalogue is the means by which available resources or objects are listed, as in a mail order catalogue. A library catalogue lists the academic resources that the library has available. This listing is not just of obvious items like books and journals but includes databases, films, DVDs, microfilm collections and anything else relevant to academic study.

In the past, the catalogue had two main purposes: to let library users know what was available and to help them locate resources in the library buildings. With the advent of online catalogues these two main purposes remain, but the functionality has been increased as users can check catalogues from a distance and do other things such as reserve and renew books. Often, access to online resources such as books and journals is via the catalogue as well, unless this is done by a separate eLibrary. It is also possible to search several library catalogues at once to locate rare or difficult to obtain material: *COPAC*, for example, searches the catalogues of nearly thirty university and national libraries in the UK, plus the specialist collections of several more (http://copac.ac.uk/).

Causal/causality

'Causation' refers to the process of one event causing or producing another event (often referred to as 'cause and effect'). A *causal relationship* between two **variables** or things – for example, smoking and major diseases – is much clearer, and far less speculative, than a **correlation** between two variables or things. A great deal of **quantitative research**, and some **qualitative research**, attempts to identify causal relationships among the variables employed in the study. In the social sciences, locating the 'cause' of something remains akin to finding a needle in a haystack.

Citations

These are the links within the text of your work that lead to the list of **references**, making it clear what is the source of your information. In the **Harvard** referencing system citations appear as an author and date in brackets: (Carroll, 2002).

Classification

Classification in respect of academic work was dealt with in Chapter 2 when we discussed the need for categorising research. Academics use all sorts of tools to attempt to parcel up the world into something understandable, for example, by using **typologies**, **concepts** and **theories**. Contrary to common belief, these classificatory tools are not for confusing the reader: the idea is to bring order to the complexity which is social life.

In respect to books and articles, classification brings together related topics and organises them in a logical and hierarchical way that aids understanding for anyone studying the subject. In practice, classification is also used to arrange books and other resources on library shelves, and the complexity of some of the systems has led to the concept gaining a bad reputation amongst students. This complexity is due to the specialised nature of academic library collections – a public library can stick little pictures of cowboy hats on its Westerns, but it is not possible to have an instantly recognisable picture that conveys 'economics of the German car industry', hence the notation HD 9710.G4 on the book spine. Online library **catalogues** are a help here as you can search by keywords.

Concept

The original meaning of the Latin term *conceptus* was 'a collecting, gathering or conceiving'. The modern-day equivalent encapsulates these sentiments. A concept is a general notion or an idea expressed in words or as a symbol. Concepts, like **theories**, range from the very simple to the complex, from the very specific to the highly abstract, and are regarded as the building blocks of theory. When concepts are operationalised in such a manner that they can be 'measured' to take on different numerical values, they are referred to as variables. Cross-border co-operation is a concept which sums up a wide variety of transboundary interaction. In a project, this concept would have to be unpacked, clarified and limited in order to make it understandable to the reader and able to be employed in research. Some concepts are notoriously slippery and difficult to define. 'Civil society', 'social capital' or the 'public sphere' are examples of concepts which attempt to capture complex social phenomena and are very hard to define precisely. Nonetheless, students need to define – as clearly as they can – the concepts they use in their essays etc.

Copyright

Copyright is intended to give authors control of the works that are their **intellectual property** and enable them to get paid for them as an encouragement to create new works and to contribute to research and learning. They, or their publishers, have exclusive rights for the publication, distribution and adaptation of the works and often the authors of the adaptation have rights as well if they make a considerable contribution. These rights also extend to the author's heirs and so books can be 'in copyright' for several years after an author's death. This period varies with the legislation of the country where works are published, but when it ends the work is in the 'public domain'.

In order to encourage the spread of ideas and knowledge there are exceptions to a completely rigid enforcement of copyright, known in UK law as 'fair dealing'. This allows the use of acknowledged quotations in reviews, academic essays, dissertations and theses. Most academic libraries display a list of what can be photocopied from books and journals under fair dealing, near the photocopiers. These rules can also apply to downloading online materials, but individual publishers can vary them as they wish. Most copyright law is rooted in the print era, but 'Creative Commons' licences are a recent development where authors can grant some rights to the public to access their works via licensing schemes.

Correlation
'Correlation' is the term used for any significant association between two or more **variables**. Importantly, correlation is not the same as 'causation'.

CSV
This stands for 'comma separated values'. It is a computer data file used to store data in a tabular form. Researchers are most likely to come across it when downloading statistics. It is by now quite old technology, but is often still used by the Office for National Statistics. CSV files can be converted into **Excel** files, or other formats, if necessary.

Data – taking care of
A mistake that almost all students and academics will make at some point in their studies is not saving their data securely by saving data in several places; such as the hard drive, a memory stick or a network drive. It takes a lot of time and effort to create your work, so you do not want to lose it. First, if you are using computers at the university and at home, make sure that they have compatible word-processing programs. Microsoft Office® 2007 can open documents created in older versions and save them in those versions, but it does not work the other way round; save it as 2007 and older programs cannot open it. There is nothing more frustrating than saving work in one format only to find that another computer is unable to decipher the rows of hieroglyphics. Second, make sure you back up your work on memory sticks and/or a network drive, so that even if your computer(s) explodes or is stolen, you still have a copy of your work to hand. Try to ensure that all versions of your work are the same, wherever they are stored – it is best to put a date on your latest version in order to prevent you working on an older, uncorrected draft. Also, save your work every few minutes in case of a crash or power cut. Record and log *all* your footnotes and bibliographical references *as you proceed*. If you manage to get into this habit, it will save you hours and nerves in the latter stages of your project. Finally, make sure you have an up-to-date virus detector on your computer(s), as a single virus could destroy hours of work.

Dependent variable
The thing which is caused or affected by the **independent variable**. In Chapter 2, we used the example of 'international prestige and a feel-good

factor' as the dependent variable, which was 'created' by the independent variable of 'government investment in elite sport' (although, as you recall, we were sceptical of this supposed causal relationship). The dependent variable is also known as the 'outcome variable', the 'endogenous variable' or the 'explanandum'. It is important to remember that every dependent variable can also be an independent variable: it is the researcher who chooses.

Digitisation

Digitisation is the process of transforming traditional information resources, including paper documents, audio and visual materials, into computer binary code, thus making them available online. By this means it is possible for an ancient manuscript in poor physical condition to be viewed by thousands with no further harm to it. Examples of major digitisation projects are Google Books and the *House of Commons Parliamentary Papers.* The downside of digitisation for researchers is that the process is often piecemeal, usually due to financial reasons. The indexing is also often overlooked as the people doing the digitising concentrate on the technical issues, which can make searching in big digitised collections a problem.

Dissertation

In the UK it is usual to use the term 'dissertation' for a relatively long piece of work over and above the length of an extended essay. Students studying for a first degree or MA usually complete a dissertation, as opposed to a **thesis** (see below). To add to the confusion, the term 'dissertation' is used in other countries, such as the US and Germany, to refer to a doctoral thesis.

Dotsam

A word modelled on the legal terms 'flotsam and jetsam', which describe wreckage from a ship, this describes wreckage on the Internet; websites, blogs and MySpace pages that were started with enthusiasm and then abandoned, and float around the Internet with outdated information. Dotsam is a nuisance when you are searching for useful material; if you are the one who created it, then it doesn't do much for your image, especially if it refers to a shady previous career that you don't want people to know about.

eBook

An eBook (or electronic book, e-book etc.) is a digital online version of a printed book, or in a very few cases it may be the only version, with no printed original. In the academic context eBooks are much more recent than eJournals and there are still a number of problems to overcome in order to make them fully integrated into the information world. Publishers often offer 'packages' of online books, rather than individual titles that are actually wanted, and then change what is available, which is a problem if you want to go back later to check something. You may also have to download extra bits of software in order to view text properly.

Many problems are associated with issues of **copyright**; the full text of a book still within copyright can only be accessed if you pay for it as an individual, or your institution pays for it. In the latter case you have to read it using your institution's eLibrary system. You can only use the special eBook reading devices that feature in the publicity for eBooks if you buy the book yourself, or download from an out-of-copyright source. The amount that can be printed out is also often less that what is allowed for photocopying of printed books.

eJournals

The 'e' stands for 'electronic', and has no drug connotations whatsoever. It refers to journals available electronically online, as opposed to those in traditional print format. In most academic disciplines this is the main way in which important research journals are accessed, because of the convenience (they are available on your computer at the click of a mouse) and the ability to search their contents using online **bibliographic databases** (also conveniently available on your computer). Another more mundane reason for their popularity is that many libraries do not have the room to display all their printed periodicals on the shelves.

eLibrary

The 'e' stands for 'electronic', as in the above cases. This is one of the names libraries use for their collections of online journals, books and databases. You often have to access these resources via the eLibrary so that your entitlement to use them can be checked, just as you have to have an ID card to enter a physical library building and borrow a book.

Empirical

From the Latin *empiricus*, meaning 'experience', empirical has come to mean the opposite of theoretical, that is, that which is derived from, guided by or based on observation, experiments or experience rather than ideas or **theories**. Many philosophical research positions and perspectives have been built up around empiricism, the core belief of which is that all knowledge is derived from sense-experience as opposed to learning through rational thinking. The term is generally used in combinations such as: empirical evidence; empirical data; empirical (as opposed to theoretical) study or research; and empirical knowledge. In the sense of 'hers was an empirical essay', the term is being employed in juxtaposition to 'theoretical', meaning the student actually drew upon or even produced **primary data**.

Epistemology

Derived from the Greek words *episteme* (knowledge) and *logos* (reason), epistemology is the **theory** of knowledge. Epistemological considerations depend on beliefs about the nature of knowledge. Well, that's cleared that up. Epistemological issues make up part of our worldview, as an epistemological debate would be about how we can know what it is we think the world is made up of (our **ontological** position). Epistemological issues are inherent in the concern about what counts as appropriate evidence in the shape of sources used in a project. Scholars differ in their assessment of what is and what is not a good source, including in-depth interviews, archival resources of long-defunct regimes, etc.

Excel

The brand name used by Microsoft for its spreadsheet application, used to store data in tabular form and therefore commonly used for statistical tables. If you are searching the Internet for statistics, Advanced Google has the facility to search for Microsoft Excel® as a file type and this can produce better results than just using 'statistics' as a search term.

Firewalls

Firewalls were originally just that: walls built to stop the spread of fire in a building; but the term now also covers measures to prevent unauthorised access to an institution's computer network. Anyone taking an academic course connected with professional development and trying to use academic resources via the computers in their workplace (such as schools or local government offices) may encounter problems with firewalls if they try to link to those resources via a **proxy server**.

Grounded theory

'Grounded theory', a phrase coined by B. G. Glaser and A. L. Strauss in the 1960s, refers to a research strategy that does not start with a **hypothesis**, but rather seeks relationships between concepts once the data have been collected. This type of research involves the interpretation of data in their social and cultural contexts.

Harvard

This is a widely used academic **referencing system**, where the **citations** in the text contain the author and publication date of the source being cited.

Thus '(Cooke, 2000: 43)' leads to the full reference: Cooke, P. (2000) *Speaking the Taboo: A Study of the Work of Wolfgang Hilbig*. Amsterdam/Atlanta: Rodopi. The use of the author and title in the citation means that Author–Date or Name–Date may be used for this referencing system.[*]

There are many variations of this style according to individual colleges and universities and it may vary even within the same institution. It is important to find out the details of how this style is applied in your institution. To add to the variety, the style varies between publishers as well. Despite the style's name, Harvard University does not act as an arbiter, or maintain a standard.

[*] *A note for purists*: to be precise, the 'Harvard' system is just one example of a *Name–Date system*; however, the specific term has now almost completely displaced the general, as with 'Hoover' and 'vacuum cleaner'. As purists will already know, this is called 'synecdoche'.

Hits

This is a slightly outdated term for the results you obtain from searching **bibliographic databases** for a particular topic. A more recent usage refers to the number of visits to a website.

HTML

HTML stands for HyperText Markup Language, and it is the computer coding behind most, but not all, web pages. Although you cannot see it on the screen, it determines the structure of online documents, making sure that line breaks, spacing, location of images etc., are all correct. Unless you are creating web pages, the only time you will be aware of it is when you are linking to the full text of an article, when you may be offered the choice between HTML and PDF.

Some people may find HTML more difficult to read, due to longer line lengths, and it may lack pagination, which can cause problems with citations and referencing. On the other hand, the HTML version can have added features, like the ability to link directly from a citation in the full text to a reference, without having to scroll down. Often, a very long document is split up into smaller sections, making it easier to find what you want.

Hypothesis

A hypothesis is a proposition, set of propositions or assumption put forward for testing; a testable proposition about the relationship between two or more events or **concepts**, for example, 'smoking' and 'cancer'. In the social world, trying to understand such causal relationships is fraught with problems, not least because we cannot emulate the laboratory conditions of the natural sciences.

Ideal type

An ideal type is a construct – a description of a phenomenon in its abstract form – which can assist in comparing and classifying specific phenomena. There is not a lot 'ideal' about it; the idea is to come up with general characteristics (e.g., of what it is to be 'working-class') to use to guide research. Such a guide would help when you engage with the literature (e.g., it could point you towards the wages people earn, their level of education, the housing they live in and so on), all of which could help build a picture of what 'working class' is made up of.

Independent variable

Shown as 'X' in formal models, the independent variable is also known as a causal variable, an explanatory variable or an exogenous variable. See **dependent variable**.

Index

'Index' comes from the same original Latin origin that also gives us the word 'indicator'. The index finger points at something and the index in a book points to where a subject can be found in the book. Indexes are basic to all academic searching and not just within books: *Applied Social Sciences Index and Abstracts* and *Social Sciences Citation Index* are just two of many that point the way from a subject to where something has been published about it in journal articles, books, conference proceedings and so on. Indexes used to be printed reference books where you looked up a term in an index volume and were referred to other volumes of the index that gave the publication details, and you then had to write the details and use the library **catalogue** to find the book or journal. **Bibliographic databases** combine the index and publication-details stages in one online search, and it is often possible to get to the full text via them as well. A book's index is a useful place to look when using the 'skimming' technique described in Chapter 2.

Institutional repositories

In the last few years many academic institutions have set up institutional repositories to preserve their intellectual output in digital format and to make it available to the wider academic community. Typically, they contain journal articles, theses and dissertations, working papers and technical reports. They are part of the **Open Access** movement, intended to make intellectual materials a more widely available resource, without the costs involved in conventional academic publishing. As a result, some of the journal articles may only be available in the pre-print version because the publisher will not allow a later one.

Intellectual property

The term 'intellectual property' covers property rights relating to the intellectual efforts put into the creation of a book, a journal article, a piece of music or a work of art. Thus a book is a piece of physical property subject to laws against it being stolen from a shop or library, whilst the ideas contained within it are intellectual property subject to laws protecting the creator from having her ideas stolen and used by someone else. In academic work these laws mainly take the form of **copyright**, although trademarks and patents are other ways of protecting intellectual property which may be encountered. **Plagiarism** is the actual theft of ideas and another person's intellectual effort, without due acknowledgement.

Internet

This term is commonly used as a synonym for the **Web**; but the Internet is actually the network of computer networks that host several other services besides the Web; including email.

IP

This can refer to **intellectual property** or to **IP addresses** (a computing term – see below).

IP addresses

An IP (Internet Protocol) address is basically a postcode for computers – although do not say that to an IT technician as they can get quite scornful about such simplifications. It enables data to be transmitted to specific addresses and allows the receiver to track the address of the sender. Publishers and suppliers of online journals and databases often use the IP address to ensure that only computers in a certain location, i.e. the institution that has paid for the resources, can receive them. To carry on the postcode analogy, your institution would be the B31 part of the code and the individual computers would be B31 5HM, B31 7GY, B31 9BF etc. – although in practice IP addresses are much longer than postcodes. Anyone with a computer that is not part of the institution's 'address' range has to make special arrangements to access this data, usually involving a **proxy server**.

JISC

This is the acronym of the Joint Information Systems Committee, which is a government-funded body responsible for developing ICT (information and communication technology) within UK higher and further education. For students and researchers the most visible sign of their work is the wide range of online materials that they make available via various projects. This includes the wealth of international statistics in *ESDS International*, and online availability of all the *House of Commons Parliamentary Papers*. *Intute*, the subject gateway to academic-quality web resources, is funded by them, as is *COPAC*, a means of searching several academic and national library catalogues simultaneously. They also provide *Hairdressing Training* which, although aimed at the vocational training sector, is notable as the UK's first freely available mobile educational service, available via handheld devices such as mobile phones.

Their website is at www.jisc.ac.uk/. This has a drop-down list of JISC services, whilst their collections of academic resources are listed at www.jisc-collections.ac.uk/.

Keyword

A keyword sums up what a document is about and is used when searching for documents in **bibliographic databases** and **subject gateways**. In addition to words in the **abstract** or summary, bibliographic databases also supply standardised keywords or subject headings that can help you find more documents about your topic if the keywords you entered did not produce many results.

Literature review

The literature review, otherwise known as a review of the literature, or literature survey, and sometimes conflated with a literature search as we do in Chapter 2, is not as straightforward as many make out. First, it is usually one of the initial steps in the research process: the review of the literature on and around the subject of enquiry. Its main functions are to avoid duplication, 'discover' gaps in research (or areas to which you can add knowledge), and 'place' your own approach among the work and approaches of other scholars. Common to all reviews is the notion of context: you set the scene for the rest of the essay/dissertation etc. An extended essay, dissertation or thesis without a literature review – without embedding or situating the student's work within the existing literature or at least discussing it – would be in serious danger of failing outright (see Chapter 2 for a lot more detail).

Methodology

Methodology is a branch of science concerned with methods and techniques of scientific enquiry; in particular, with investigating the potential and limitations of particular techniques or procedures. The term pertains to the science and study of methods and the assumptions about the ways in which knowledge is produced. A certain methodological approach will be underpinned by, and reflect, specific **ontological** and **epistemological** assumptions. These assumptions will determine the *choice* of approach and methods adopted in a given study by emphasising particular ways of knowing and finding out about the world. Methodology deals with the logic of enquiry, of how **theories** can be generated and subsequently tested. Methodology is *very* often confused and used interchangeably with **methods**.

Methods

The original Greek meaning of 'method' was 'the pursuit of knowledge'. In a sense, this is still what it means in research today, in as much as the methods a researcher employs in a study, that is, the techniques and procedures used to collect and analyse data, are the tools with which we pursue knowledge. There is a wide variety of methods, ranging from discourse analysis, archival retrieval of data, interviews, direct observation, comparisons of data, and documentary analysis, to surveys, questionnaires and statistics. Certain methods can be used in either **qualitative** or **quantitative research**. Although there is a general and artificial division between the two types of approach, the best social science research is often carried out using a combination of both. The methods employed in a project are usually informed by the methodology chosen and the questions asked, rather than the other way around.

Netiquette

A term created by combining the words 'net' and 'etiquette'. It describes a number of norms and behaviour that are intended to regulate how people deal with each other online; in emails, blogs and so forth. Without the many clues as to how other people are reacting that are present in face-to-face situations there are unfortunately plenty of opportunities for misunderstandings to occur and offence to be taken. Netiquette tries to ensure standards of politeness and professionalism, and the reputation of anyone ignoring it will suffer.

Numbering

Numbering is a reference system that uses numbers for the citations within the text, which refer you to a references list that may appear as footnotes, or at the end of the chapter, or of the whole work. The system is also sometimes called Numeric of Vancouver.

Off-campus access

This expression may well appear in the information given by the library or the IT people in your institution. It does not refer to gaining access via the

Internet. It does refer to the problem of getting access to online journals and other resources where publishers have restricted access to computers with an **IP address** range within the institution that has paid for those online resources. Solutions for this include using a **proxy server**, but always read the advice given by your institution as to what they do.

Online
Like a lot of computer terms this has a specific technical meaning and a much more widely used one; in this case when used as a description of anything available on the **Internet** or the World Wide **Web**.

Ontology
Ontology is a branch of metaphysics concerned with the nature of being. The first part of the word comes from the Greek verb equivalent to the English 'to be'. It can be understood as the basic image of social reality upon which a **theory** is based. It can, however, be better understood as the way in which we view the world; it is our starting point in research, upon which the rest of the process is based. Ontological claims are 'claims and assumptions that are made about the nature of social reality, claims about what exists, what it looks like, what units make it up and how these units interact with each other. In short, ontological assumptions are concerned with what we believe constitutes social reality' (Blaikie, 2000: 8). Your 'ontological position', whether you know it or not, is implicit even before you choose your topic of study. We all have views on how the world is made up and what the most important components of the social world are.

Open Access
Open Access is free online access to academic publications. Many conventional publishers also publish open access journals, and universities and colleges often support publication from their own resources. They also often have **institutional repositories**, which make their intellectual output, in the form of journal article preprints, theses, working papers and so on, available free online.

Paradigm
Originally meaning 'pattern' or 'model', 'paradigm' has come to mean, broadly, 'an established academic approach' in a specific discipline in which academics use a common terminology, and generally draw on common **theories**, which in turn employ agreed **methods** and practices. Paradigms, which act as organising frameworks for researchers, are often overtaken or replaced by others, leading to what is commonly called a 'paradigm shift',

that is, the former majority approach is superseded by a new approach, using different terminology, theories, methods and practices. In this book we have generally reserved the term 'paradigm' to distinguish between research traditions.

Paraphrasing

The art of summarising an author's views and opinions in your own words, whilst at the same time crediting the author via a **citation** within the text so that whoever reads your work can check the original source for themselves. If paraphrasing is done by a cut and paste of the original, with no indication of who is being paraphrased, then it is **plagiarism**.

PDF

Portable Document Format (PDF) is a major means of making documents available on the Web; the documents look exactly the same as the 'original' printed versions, with the pagination of the print version and a layout that some may find easier to read than **HTML**.

PDF is a relatively simple means of getting a lot of published text online very quickly and it is consequently popular with governments, who can say they are making information 'publicly available'. However, downloading and searching within government reports that may be several hundred pages long has practical drawbacks for the researcher. Look out for something described as 'searchable PDF' as the text within it can be searched with keywords. Many journal publishers have a fondness for using the very latest versions of PDF and if you do not have this version on your computer you get blank pages. With software companies being the way they are, you will probably get a little reminder to download the required version.

Plagiarism

The word 'plagiarism' derives from the Latin for kidnapper, but as a crime it is really closer to a mixture of theft and fraud; the theft of someone's ideas that is then passed off as the plagiariser's own efforts in their work without due acknowledgement. In academia this can be looked upon as the crime of all crimes, given that generating ideas is central to the purpose of such an institution.

Positivism and Interpretivism

'Positivism' is a very broad term under which many different approaches to social enquiry are known. Positivist researchers believe in a 'truth' that can be uncovered and they seek to do so by, usually, using quantitative methods, causal explanations and even the 'prediction' of human behaviour.

Interpretivism, on the other hand, is an approach to social enquiry that has developed in opposition to positivism. The reason why so many authors choose to outline positivism and interpretivism – and thereby leave out a whole host of social research between these binary poles – is because they can be seen as opposites: positivists seek objectivity while interpretivists believe in subjectivity; positivists tend to model their research on the natural sciences while interpretivists believe there is a clear distinction to be made between the natural and the social world, and therefore we need a methodology and methods of gathering data that are more in tune with the subjects we are studying. Interpretivist researchers do not believe in any one 'truth'; they generally seek to uncover the beliefs of the actors they study and their understanding of the context in which they operate, and they do not believe in predicting human behaviour (see Grix, 2010, chapter 5).

Primary materials/data/sources
See **Sources**.

Provenance
'Provenance' was originally a term used in the art world relating to the origin and authenticity of an art work. Such a work would have a detailed listing of every previous owner, with evidence, so that there was a clear line of origin back to the original artistic creator. The term can also be used for the origin of ideas and theories. With printed books and journals you usually have some clues as to *who* created something (author), *when* they did it (publication date), and this is a good start for assessing *why* they created it. With the Internet and the copy and paste culture these clues become more tenuous and web-based sources have to be subjected to severe intellectual scrutiny to ascertain their provenance and therefore their academic worth. (Anyone who has read the rest of this book will notice that Kipling's Honest Serving-Men have popped up again – hard-working little chaps aren't they?)

Proxy servers
These are the main means of dealing with the problem of **off-campus access** to journals and databases where the publishers have restricted access to an academic institution's range of **IP addresses** and the computer you are using has an IP address outside that range. You adjust the settings on whichever Internet browser you use so that you can use the proxy server (which has an IP address in the correct range) to receive data from the publishers. Only people registered with the institution can register for the proxy service.

Proxy servers slow down your Internet connection, so it is advisable to switch the proxy service off when not using your computer to look at eJournals and databases.

Some institutions are installing software that removes the need for individuals to adjust their browsers when using the proxy server; they are logged in to the proxy when they use their institutional username and password. Although things are simpler for the end user, the basic rerouting via a server with the correct IP address remains.

Qualitative research

'Qualitative' is derived from 'quality', a term coined by Plato to mean 'of what kind'. Qualitative research is characterised by the use of methods that attempt to examine 'inherent traits, characteristics, and qualities of the [political] objects of inquiry' (Landman, 2000: 227). The **methods** used in this type of research tend to be more interpretative in nature. However, the simplistic dichotomy of 'qualitative' methods = the interpretivist paradigm and 'quantitative' methods = the positivist paradigm should be avoided, as researchers from both research **paradigms** use an array of research methods.

Quantitative research

This term is derived from 'quantity', and pertains to numbers. Quantitative research employs methods with the intention of being able to produce data that can be quantified (counted, measured, weighed, enumerated, and so manipulated and compared mathematically). This type of research is interested in finding general patterns and relationships among **variables**, testing **theories** and even making predictions.

Quotations

Quotations are exact copies of phrases or sentences taken from your original source and incorporated into your work. It is very important to make sure that your readers know when this occurs, to avoid any suggestion of **plagiarism**. Short quotations are indicated with quotation marks (" ") and longer ones by being indented from the main text; in both cases you need a **citation** leading to a **reference** that gives details of the source. Another important point about quotations is that they are intended to illustrate or support your own arguments; padding out an essay with long quotations will not go down well, even if they are properly cited and referenced.

Reference-management software

This is software that you use to manage (i.e. keep track of) the references you use in your work. It is a computerised version of the boxes of index cards that researchers used to use. However, it goes beyond just keeping track of what you have read or found in literature searches – because it is computerised you can use it to insert and format references into your work in the style used by your institution.

There are various proprietary brands of reference-management software and different ways of gaining access to them. Some, such as EndNote and Reference Manager, are downloaded onto public computers at your institution or onto your own if you buy your own copy. Others, such as RefWorks, are networked online, but you can only access them if your institution has paid for them. In order to use the facility to insert and format references into your text, word processing and the reference-management software have to be on the same computer, so if you are using a public terminal you need to remember to bring your own file of references with you on a portable device like a memory stick (and not lose it!).

References

References give details of all the sources you have used in your work. **Citations** within the text enable whoever is reading it to go to the reference and locate the original work. They can then form their own opinion of what you have said about the original, or use it in their own work. There are standardised **referencing systems** to ensure that all relevant details, such as author, date, title, page number etc., are included in a consistent format.

Referencing systems

Referencing systems are used to provide a consistent format for recording the details of the work produced by others that you mention in your work and to enable others to refer to that work. The most widely used system is called **Harvard** or Author–Date or even Name–Date and is the one used by the authors of this book; it is also used for the examples in the chapter on referencing.

You may encounter other systems such as the 'Humanities' or 'Numeric' method, which involves the citation of references by a superscript numeral in the text, with the full bibliographical details of the work given in the footnote text at the bottom of the page or in endnotes at the end of the section or chapter.

Referencing systems are based on the conventions of printed works and now have to be adapted to newer formats, for example by including **URLs** and the date accessed, in references for material found on websites. Square brackets [ ] are a useful convention for indicating extra details that you have added because they help locate the resource, even if they are not part of the original referencing system.

Research questions

Research questions are intended to guide your enquiries. By establishing general research questions, the researcher begins to narrow her focus of enquiry, something that is essential given the amount of information available. 'Why do governments invest in elite sport?' is a legitimate research question and one that cannot simply be answered with a 'yes' or 'no'.

Search engines

Search engines are one way of searching the Web for resources on a topic. To be able to search such a vast amount of data, most of them rely heavily on automated searching. As a result they often miss out on the subtleties of human language, where one word can mean different things in different contexts. In addition they do not take into account the academic level of the search; school children's homework and a Master's dissertation are all the same to them. In some cases search engines have some human input to try to fine-tune them and lessen the crudities; thus trying to make them more like the other way of searching the Internet, via **subject gateways**.

Self-plagiarism

Submitting the same piece of work for two or more assignments is self-plagiarism and is just as dishonest as passing off someone else's work as your own. Plagiarism-checking software compares current work from an individual with their earlier work, so it can detect it. If you feel there was a real gem in your earlier work you can still reuse it later, as long as you quote and reference yourself properly and give the original source of the gem.

SFX

This is the computer software that links, amongst other things, the summary of a journal article in a **bibliographic database** to the full text of the article in an **eJournal**, even though that may be from a completely different publisher. The sort of thing you take for granted until it goes wrong, and you are not taken to the full text you expected.

Shibboleth

'Shibboleth' is the name of the new password system for gaining access to academic online resources; it replaced **Athens** for most of these resources in the Summer of 2008. For most of the time you are not aware of it as you use your institutional username and password, and the only clue is the word 'Shibboleth' flashing on the screen when moving between resources. Occasionally there is a glitch and you will be asked to select something like the 'Access Management Federation' in order to get access.

'Shibboleth' is not easy to say, and in the Old Testament it was used as a test to separate Hebrews (who could pronounce 'th') from their foes (who couldn't), hence its modern usage for a password system.

Sources

Sources are crucial to the research process. They represent the evidence with which to test **theories**, propositions, hunches, and so on. Without **empirical** evidence in the form of, for example, documents, statistics, interview transcripts etc., **research questions** and **hypotheses** in the social and human sciences would remain unanswered and untested, an unsatisfactory state of affairs unless the purpose of research was to contribute to theoretical debates. There is no general transdisciplinary consensus on the usefulness of some sources as opposed to others, as is the case with **methods**, **methodologies**, perspectives and theories. However, the theoretical underpinnings of your project will have a great impact on which sources you will use. Generally, a wide source base will lessen the chance of an invalid study. Sources come in many shapes and sizes: primary sources are usually those generated by the researcher herself (i.e. interview transcripts, survey results) or unpublished materials dug up by the researcher (i.e. archival papers etc.). Secondary sources are deemed those sources collected by or written by others, for example, books and articles. For college and undergraduate students, most institutions do not expect the use of primary sources, although for advanced undergraduates this should be actively encouraged, as learning about 'methods' and 'methodology' only really makes sense when applied in real-world research.

Stacks

Traditional academic libraries often tended to have two types of space: reading rooms with lofty ceilings and good lighting; and stacks, with neither. Unfortunately it was the latter that tended to house (and often still do house) the journals and books needed for research.

Subject gateways

Subject gateways are a means of searching the Internet to find resources suitable for use at an academic level. They originated in the early days of the Internet with individual academics and librarians creating their own lists of useful sites. The three characteristics of subject gateways, both then and now, are that they depend on human thought and judgement, they are subject focused, and they exclude material not suitable for inclusion in academic work. These points differentiate them from the other way of searching the Internet, via **search engines**.

Subject headings
See **Keywords**.

Theory
There are many different types of theory, ranging from grand and middle-range to **grounded theory**. The difference between theories is their degree of abstraction and their scope. Grand theory is very abstract and presents a conceptual scheme 'intended to represent the important features of a total society' (Blaikie, 2000: 144). Middle-range theories, probably the most commonly used in research, are limited to a specific domain, for example, the labour process (Bryman, 2001: 6). A theory is a guess about the way things are. Theories are abstract notions which assert specific relationships between **concepts**. In research, theories are linked to *explanation* as opposed to *description*. The abstract ideas and propositions contained in theory are generally tested in fieldwork by the collection of data. A good theory will be generalisable and able to be employed in different contexts from the original. In the words of Karl Popper, theories are 'nets cast to catch what we call 'the world': to rationalise, to explain and to master it. We endeavour to make the mesh ever finer and finer' (Popper, 2000: 59).

All research is theoretical, whether it wants to be or not, because a person who suggests they are 'simply getting on with the job of research by starting with some empirical data or documents' has, without knowing it, made a number of assumptions about research, the methods they are using and the sources the methods produce.

Thesis
A thesis is the large body of written work necessary for gaining a PhD or MPhil. The former usually requires a work of between 80,000 and 120,000 words, whereas the latter usually requires between 20,000 and 60,000 words.

Time management
There are only a set number of hours in a day and yet you need to fit in your studies (and for some, perhaps a part-time job), and even a social life. Time management is a technique for getting as much done in as short a time as possible without getting overstressed and without cutting corners and sacrificing quality. Starting an essay the day before it is due, and copying and pasting chunks off a website to get it finished, is the worst possible time management. Oddly enough, time management does involve some initial investment of extra time; planning timetables, careful note taking so you don't waste time later looking up references, and so on.

Universities and colleges often run courses or give advice on time manage-ment, and it is a useful skill to take with you when you venture out into the world of work.

Typology

The early Greek philosophers Socrates, Plato and Aristotle all used some form of categorisation. Today, a typology, like a taxonomy, can be seen as a classificatory system with which the researcher categorises data. These devices can be seen as loose frameworks with which to organise and systematise our observations. Like **ideal types**, typologies and taxonomies do not necessarily provide us with explanation, rather they describe empiri-cal phenomena by fitting them into a set of categories, which, of course, may aid subsequent explanation.

URL

The Uniform Resource Locator (URL) is the address of a website that appears in the box at the top of the screen. If the highly IT-literate find this an inade-quate definition, that's just tough, it works for most of us. The URL can contain useful information about the site; for example, British academic websites have '.ac.uk' in the address, whilst American ones have '.edu'.

Variables

Variables are concepts which vary in amount or kind. Researchers opera-tionalise **concepts** by translating them into variables that can be 'measured' and used in gathering information.

Web

'The Web' is the common name for the World Wide Web (the www within a **URL**). It is often used as a synonym for the **Internet**, but it is actually just one of the services available on the Internet.

Web-based

Anything available on the **Web**.

Wikis

A wiki is a collaborative website where all who access it can edit the contents; by far the best known major example is *Wikipedia*. Doubts are often expressed about the reliability of this as it is so easy for people to add their own malicious and inaccurate data to the system. Even if this is spotted there is the even bigger problem of anonymity, which make evaluation of worth very difficult: without knowing *who* is creating an entry it is difficult to establish a meaningful answer to *why* they are doing it or *how* they have come by the information. On a much smaller scale, wiki technology is used as an intranet within organisations, and these can be much more valuable as they are less prone to sabotage. It is also possible to have wikis that give the names of the editors and contributors, thus lending them an authenticity and validity that they would otherwise lack.

Bibliography

Aristotle (1948) *Politics*, ed. E. Baker (Oxford: Clarendon Press).

Bank holiday (2009) (http://en.wikipedia.org/wiki/Bank_holiday [accessed 11 February 2009]).

Bell, J. (1993) *Doing Your Research Project: A Guide to First-Time Researchers in Education and Social Science* (Buckingham: Open University Press).

Blaikie, N. (2000) *Designing Social Research* (Cambridge: Polity).

Brabazon, T. (2007) *The University of Google: Education in the (Post) Information Age* (Aldershot: Ashgate).

Bryman, A. (2001) *Social Research Methods* (Oxford: Oxford University Press).

Buckler, S. and Dolowitz, D. (2005) *Politics on the Internet: A Student's Guide* (London: Routledge).

Carr-Hill, R. (2005) 'Evidence and Development: Poverty, Literacy, HIV', in *ESDS International Conference 2005, 2 November 2005, London* (www.esds.ac.uk/international/documents/conf2005rch.ppt [accessed 29 April 2009]).

Cashmore, E. (2003) *Making Sense of Sports*, 3rd edition (London/New York: Routledge).

Caulkin, S. (2006) 'Why things fell apart for joined-up thinking', *Observer* [unpaginated] (www.guardian.co.uk/society/2006/feb/26/publicservices. politics [accessed 11 August 2008]).

Department for Culture, Media and Sport (DCMS) (2002) 'Game Plan, a Strategy for Delivering Government's Sport and Physical Activity Objectives', produced by the DCMS and the Strategy Unit.

Encyclopaedia Britannica (2006) (http://corporate.britannica.com/ britannica_nature_response.pdf [accessed 9 June 2008]).

Esping-Andersen, G. (1990) *The Three Worlds of Welfare Capitalism* (Cambridge: Polity Press).

Fairbairn, G. J. and Winch, C. (2000) *Reading, Writing and Reasoning: A Guide for Students* (Buckingham/Philadelphia: Open University Press).

Giles, J. (2005) 'Internet Encyclopaedias Go Head to Head', *Nature*, 438: 900–1.

Grix, J. (1998) 'Competing Approaches to the Collapse of the GDR: "Top-Down" *vs.* "Bottom-Up"', *Journal of Area Studies*, Issue 13, Revolutions (Special Issue), pp. 121–42.

Grix, J. (2001) 'Social Capital as a Concept in the Social Sciences: the State of the Debate', *Democratization*, 8 (3), pp. 189–210.

Grix, J. (2009) 'The Impact of UK Sport Policy on the Governance of Athletics', in *International Journal of Sport Policy*, 1 (1) (March 2009), pp. 31–49.

Grix, J. (2010) *Foundations of Research*, 2nd edn (Basingstoke: Palgrave Macmillan).

Grix, J. and Lacroix, C. (2006) 'Constructing Germany's Image in the British Press: an Empirical Analysis of Stereotypical Reporting on Germany', *Journal of Contemporary European Studies*, 14 (3) (Dec. 2006), pp. 373–92.

Hart, C. (2000) *Doing a Literature Review* (London: Sage).

Heywood, A. (2002) *Politics* (Basingstoke: Palgrave Macmillan).

Hodgson, S. M. and Irving, Z. (eds) (2007) *Policy Reconsidered: Meanings, Politics and Practices* (Bristol: Policy Press).

Internet Detective (2009) (www.vts.intute.ac.uk/detective [accessed 21 July 2009]).

Jacso, P. (2005) 'Google Scholar (Redux)', *Peter's digital reference shelf*, June [unpaginated] (www2.hawaii.edu/~jacso/ [select Publications, select Peter's Digital Reference Shelf and title of article] [accessed 10 July 2008]).

Jenkins, R. (2008) 'TV Psychiatrist Raj Persaud Suspended for Plagiarism', *Times online* 21 June 2008 [unpaginated] (www.timesonline.co.uk/tol/news/uk/article4179597.ece [accessed 4 December 2008]).

King's College London (2006) 'Statement regarding Dr Raj Persaud', *King's College London News Archive*, 12 April 2006 [unpaginated] (www.kcl.ac.uk/news/news_details_2006.php?news_id=43 [accessed 4 December 2008]).

Kipling, R. (1940) *Rudyard Kipling's Verse* (London: Hodder & Stoughton; definitive edition).

Kuhn, T. S. (1996) *The Structure of Scientific Revolutions* (Chicago/London: University of Chicago Press).

Landman, T. (2000) *Issues and Methods in Comparative Politics: An Introduction* (London/Thousand Oaks/New Dehli: Sage).

National Register of Archives (2009) *Questions about the Cabinet Secretaries' Notebooks* (www.nationalarchives.gov.uk/releases/2009/march/questions.htm [accessed 26 March 2009]).

Nature (2006) 'Encyclopaedia Britannica and *Nature*: a Response', 23 March 2006 [Press release] (www.nature.com/press_releases/Britannica response.pdf [accessed 9 June 2008]).

Phipps, L. (2008) *Research 2.0? Risks and Rewards of Using Emergent Technologies* [unpaginated; PowerPoint slide numbers used in citations] (http://lawrie.jiscinvolve.org/2008/05/11/research-20-risks-and-rewards-of-using-emergent-technologies/ [accessed 7 July 2008]).

Popper, K. (2000) *The Logic of Scientific Discovery* (London/New York: Routledge).

Plato (1994) *Republic*, trans. Robin Waterfield (Oxford/New York: Oxford University Press).

Sturcke, J. and Wainwright, M. (2008) 'Disgraced Raj Persaud Quits as Consultant at Leading Hospital', *Guardian.co.uk*, 24 October 2008 [unpaginated] (www.guardian.co.uk/lifeandstyle/2008/oct/24/raj-persaud-psychiatry-maudsley [accessed 4 December 2008]).

Suber, P. (2002) 'Analogies and Precedents for the FOS Revolution', *Free Online Scholarship (FOS) Newsletter*, 11 March 2002 [unpaginated] (www.earlham.edu/~peters/fos/newsletter/03-11-02.htm#analogies [accessed 18 July 2008]).

UK Statistics Authority (2008) *Earlier Census, 1801–1991* (www.statistics.gov.uk/census2001/earlier_censuses.asp [accessed 24 July 2009]).

Index

Note: Page numbers in **bold** refer to definitions or explanations within the Glossary.